adult adhd executive function 7-week power-up

YOUR TOOLKIT TO ENHANCE FOCUS, MANAGE TIME, AND BOOST PRODUCTIVITY EFFECTIVELY FOR A FULFILLING LIFE

ESTELLE ROSE

ROSALI PUBLISHING

Connie Newell

★★★★★ **Transformative resource!**
Reviewed in the United States on October 21, 2024

"A true gem for anyone navigating life with ADHD. Rose's approach is warm, encouraging, and deeply affirming, making you feel seen and understood. Highly recommended for anyone looking for both guidance and a sense of community in the pages of a book. I walked away feeling more empowered and equipped to handle the unique challenges ADHD presents."

Lizelle

★★★★★ **A Surprisingly Eye-Opening Guide, Even for a Skeptic**
Reviewed in the United States on October 25, 2024
Verified Purchase

"To my surprise, this 2-in-1 guide was not just a dry self-help manual. It was practical, down-to-earth, and very easy to follow, even for someone like me who avoids this genre. The emotional insights really hit home."

Glitter

★★★★★ **A Game-Changer for Women with ADHD**
Reviewed in the United States on October 20, 2024
Verified Purchase

"I often feel like the advice out there doesn't really fit my life. This book? It totally gets it. I've been able to go through the exercises at my own pace, and I feel like I'm actually making progress with my executive function and self-regulation. Plus, it's refreshing that the book doesn't make me feel bad about having ADHD."

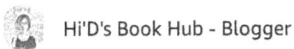 Hi'D's Book Hub - Blogger

★★★★★ **Embrace your uniqueness!**
Reviewed in the United States on October 22, 2024
Verified Purchase

"After reading Estelle Rose's book, I felt a genuine connection to her and others like me. She taught me how to apply certain insights from the book to my daily life. I appreciated that it wasn't just a book but also a workbook designed to enhance my understanding."

 dorianhellfire

★★★★★ **So helpful and relatable**
Reviewed in the United States on October 20, 2024
Verified Purchase

"Thank you for making this book! As someone who's discovering what it means to live with ADHD, this book has been a wonder to have."

 Aleisha Wilhite

★★★★★ **Helpful book**
Reviewed in the United States on August 28, 2024
Verified Purchase

"If I could sum up the book's essence in one word it would be EYE-opening. I found the budgeting tips and empowering money chapters very transformative as I am also an impulsive spender."

 Megan Wilson

★★★★★ **Life-Changing**
Reviewed in the United States on October 23, 2024
Verified Purchase

"The author's tone made reading this book easy and fun. Since she has ADHD herself, I found it to be relatable, funny, and encouraging. I'm grateful for the work she's doing to help women like me and hopeful that it (and hopefully additional research, studies, and books) will make navigating life with ADHD easier for girls and women in future generations."

 Tay

Exceptional writing and author!
Reviewed in the United States on April 14, 2024
Verified Purchase

"I really appreciate how the author was able to put so much in this book, she is personable and relatable. The book is very easy to read and understand. Where was this book when I was in grade school? Definitely one of the best self-help books I have read."

 Briony Anderson

The only book for ADHD I'll read
Reviewed in Australia on 28 July 2023
Verified Purchase

"This book is many things to me. Comforting and relatable yet super informative and full of helping, healthy, evidence based tips to assist with emotional dysfunction, eating habits and even impulsivity. I love how Estelle talks not only about why implementing some of these changes can be beneficial, she also provides step by step instructions and resources you can follow to actually stay motivated in keeping these healthy changes."

 Sarah Byington

Friendly & Engaging Guide to Managing ADHD
Reviewed in the United States on August 21, 2023
Verified Purchase

"This book has been a great resource for navigating my ADHD. It is written in a friendly tone that that makes it easy to read and I didn't feel bombarded by too much information at a time. The illustrations are a helpful addition. I liked how balanced it felt between science backed information and anecdotal stories."

 G. Wagstaff

Most helpful book I've read about ADHD
Reviewed in the United Kingdom on 15 February 2024
Verified Purchase

"All I can say is that as I was reading this book, I felt like Estelle was actually talking to me. And trying to help me. I keep this book handy because I dip into it whenever I feel like I'm all over the place (which is quite often). It grounds me. Thank you, Estelle."

 Catherine S

☆☆☆☆☆ **Basically seeing someone write my life!**
Reviewed in the United Kingdom on 5 January 2024
Verified Purchase

"I am not a reader - I just don't have the concentration to read. I read this book in a few hours; this never happens! I bought this book because I guess... hyperfixation of my recent ADHD diagnosis. The tools I feel will be helpful for me (I spoke to my partner) and we're going to try some of them around organising this weekend. Fingers crossed!"

 Neate-Neate

☆☆☆☆☆ **This book felt like a friend helping me**
Reviewed in the United Kingdom on 21 November 2023
Verified Purchase

"I decided to only buy 2 books about ADHD (because of money and because i can get carried away) and so I did my research as they had to be good ones. This book was spot on."

 Tina

☆☆☆☆☆ **Great intro to ADHD**
Reviewed in Canada on July 28, 2023
Verified Purchase

"This book is written in such a user friendly and engaging way. I found it very helpful as someone new to ADHD and trying to learn as much as possible as quickly as possible. This book is a great starting off point with lots of helpful examples of lived experience and ideas on how to adapt to challenges."

Copyright © 2025 by Estelle Rose - All rights reserved.

No part of this publication may be reproduced, stored or transmitted in any form or by any means, electronic, mechanical, photocopying, recording, scanning, or otherwise without written permission from the publisher. It is illegal to copy this book, post it to a website, or distribute it by any other means without permission. Estelle Rose asserts the moral right to be identified as the author of this work.

This book is copyright protected. This book is only for personal use. You cannot amend, distribute, sell, use, quote or paraphrase any part, or the content within this book, without the consent of the author or publisher.

Under no circumstances will any blame or legal responsibility be held against the publisher, or author, for any damages, reparation, or monetary loss due to the information contained within this book. Either directly or indirectly. You are responsible for your own choices, actions, and results.

Designations used by companies to distinguish their products are often claimed as trademarks. All brand names and product names used in this book and on its cover are trade names, service marks, trademarks and registered trademarks of their respective owners. The publishers and the book are not associated with any product or vendor mentioned in this book. None of the companies referenced within the book have endorsed the book.

Please note the information contained within this document is for educational and entertainment purposes only. All effort has been executed to present accurate, up to date, and reliable, complete information. No warranties of any kind are declared or implied. Readers acknowledge that the author is not engaging in the rendering of legal, financial, medical or professional advice. The content within this book has been derived from various sources. Please consult a licensed professional before attempting any techniques outlined in this book.

By reading this document, the reader agrees that under no circumstances is the author responsible for any losses, direct or indirect, which are incurred as a result of the use of the information contained within this document, including, but not limited to, — errors, omissions, or inaccuracies.

First edition

contents

Introduction	ix
How To Use This Book	xiii
WEEK 1: ADHD, EXECUTIVE FUNCTION, AND YOU	1
Mapping the journey ahead	
WEEK 2: TRAIN YOUR BRAIN	21
Sharpen Memory, Focus and Attention	
WEEK 3: FLEX YOUR NEURONS	39
How to Find Relief with Cognitive Flexibility	
WEEK 4: MASTERING SPACE	53
5 ADHD-Friendly Principles to Create a Space That Works for You	
Week 5: MASTERING TIME BEYOND THE CLOCK	69
How to Find Bliss in Time Management	
WEEK 6: HEALTHY PRODUCTIVITY	83
How to Achieve Goals Without Burnouts	
WEEK 7: EMOTION REGULATION AND IMPULSIVITY	105
How to Proceed Mindfully	
In Conclusion	127
Resources	131
About the Author	134
Also by Estelle Rose	136
Bibliography	139

introduction

What am I doing here? Wait, why did I come into the kitchen again? Hold on, I was just at my desk, working... I swear I had a reason for walking in here. Oh, come on, think... Nope! Gone! Am I turning into a goldfish?

Alright, take a deep breath. Let's backtrack: I was at my desk, doing something... Nope, nothing. I guess I'll just go back to work.

Now, where was I? Let's check my to-do list on my phone. *Oh, hey, there's a notification. Oh, it's Mandy! She's asking if I'm free on Saturday.* That's nice, I haven't seen her in ages. *Oh, I'm thirsty! Let me grab a glass of water. Okay, kitchen. Glass. No glasses in the cupboard. Ugh, I forgot to run the dishwasher last night. Fine, I'll just wash one up.*

Oh, the sink is full. So depressing. I'm such a slob. Never mind, I'll drink from a jar, pretend I'm cool! No, I hate the feeling of drinking from a jar, the rim, the shape, the thickness. I'll just grab a mug instead. Okay, mug... tea... kettle. Let's put the kettle on. While that's boiling, I'll just check my email...

One hour later...

I'm thirsty. Oh, my tea is cold. Wait! I never even got that glass of water.

Does this sound familiar? Are you constantly trying to remember your last thought, only to get pulled in a dozen different directions? Does your to-do list feel like a never-ending conveyor belt of half-finished tasks, each taunting you with stress and frustration as new distractions constantly pop up?

I get it. Believe me, I feel this in my bones. What you're experiencing is called executive dysfunction, the number one villain in the ADHD movie of our lives. Yes, I've got ADHD too. But here's the thing: I'm also a productivity nerd, an empowerment coach, and I've learned that while productivity hacks are great, they don't fix everything. Not by a long shot.

For years, I crammed my life full of every productivity trick in the book. I became the queen of planning, organizing, and getting stuff done—even with undiagnosed ADHD. On paper, I had it all: the creative career, the family, the community involvement. I even taught others how to be productive and chase their dreams. And I did it well, if I say so myself.

But what I didn't realize was the toll it was taking. I was burnt out, struggling to connect with my emotions, feeling like I couldn't string two thoughts together, let alone care for others or plan for my future. That's when I fully understood the meaning of the expression "you can't pour from an empty cup"—and that no amount of productivity tools could fix executive dysfunction without addressing the deeper issues.

So, what's executive function, anyway? If your brain fog is thicker than Victorian London and you've ever wandered into the kitchen and forgotten why, that's your working memory letting you down.

Can't stay on task? That's ADHD's signature "squirrel syndrome" and general scatterbrain tendencies. What else? Do you find yourself blurting out during conversations or buying shiny objects you don't really need? Yep, that's poor impulse control at work.

But there is more. There is also time blindness. Do you hyperfocus and lose track of time? Maybe it spirals into chronic lateness? Or perhaps you constantly underestimate how long something takes, which makes your to-do list as long as the Great Wall of China and makes you edge dangerously into burnout.

Yes, I know. I've been there, too. By geeking out on productivity, I forced myself to conform to society's hyper-achieving expectations, which left me overwhelmed, fatigued, and unable to function.

That's the thing about productivity hacks: they can work, but only if you're also addressing the root cause of executive dysfunction. Without that, they can leave our neurospicy brains feeling more inadequate than ever.

But here's the good news—there's a better way. Yes, I will share my favorite productivity tools, specially tailored for ADHD brains. But I'll also show you how to pick the ones that bring calm, not chaos, and create a fulfilling life without running on a hamster wheel.

This book is about more than just productivity. Enhanced productivity is only the tip of executive functioning with ADHD. Over the next seven weeks, we'll dive into a full executive function power-up. You'll discover proven cognitive behavior techniques to sharpen your working memory, focus, and attention. You will flex your cognitive muscles, and learn to master time and space better than a time-travelling superhero. We'll tackle impulse control and emotional regulation, empowering you to take control in ways that actually stick.

How does that sound? This is a buffet of executive function tools where you get to help yourself seven times to pick and choose the strategies that work for your unique life, needs, and definition of fulfillment.

And don't worry, this isn't a one-size-fits-all approach. Whether you're a top executive, a self-employed artist, an ER nurse, or a single stay-at-home parent crumbling under the mental load, we'll find the right tools for *you*.

Let me guess. Have you ever packed your diary full, telling yourself this time would be different—that you'd stick to the plan, tick all the boxes, and finally get everything done? You probably dove in with the best intentions, only to stop a few days (or weeks) later, feeling like you failed yet again. I get it. I've been there too.

That's the problem with most productivity advice: it relies solely on external solutions—planners, schedules, apps—and expects you to magically transform overnight. But real, lasting change doesn't happen that way. Why? Because transformation can't come from outside alone, and you can't trick your way through executive functioning.

In my early days as a coach, I helped young professionals land their dream jobs. I gave them all the external tools they needed—planning, prioritizing, goal-setting, and so on. And while those tools helped, I quickly realized that the real, sustainable change came when they started working on themselves from the inside out.

And that's where this book is different. Many books only offer the external solutions—planners, techniques, checklists. But this book takes a dual approach, working both from the outside in and the inside out. Yes, you'll get the practical tools and plenty of quick wins to organize your life, manage your time, and get things done. But you'll also learn how to cultivate the internal shift necessary to make those tools stick.

We'll dig into the deep stuff—the emotional regulation, the impulse control, the scattered thoughts—while also exploring why those external tools haven't worked for you in the past. Because once you align your external tools with your internal transformation, that's when the magic happens. This book doesn't just slap a band-aid on executive dysfunction; it helps you build real, sustainable change starting with a 7-week power-up...

So, the buffet is laid out. I set the table, chose my best linen, arranged the flowers, and lit the candles. Will you stay for the seven-course meal?

how to use this book

DISCLAIMER

All the tools and strategies here are shared for educational purposes. I am not a medical doctor and share my experience as a fellow ADHDer and a coach who's been nerding down on the subject. As mentioned in all of my other books, this book does not replace a professional diagnosis, treatment, or therapy. It's *in addition to*, not *instead of*. Never hesitate to get medical help when you need it.

HOW TO READ THIS BOOK?

You can read this book as intended: one week at a time, taking time to select your tools and put them into action. Or, if you can't wait to see all the goodies I've got in stock for you and you want to know where we're heading, you can read it all in one go and then come back to select and apply the tools one week at a time.

DOES IT NEED TO BE SEVEN WEEKS?

Love your inquisitive spirit!

Seven weeks is a reasonable amount of time; it keeps you on your toes by making the pace and the transformation fast enough for our impatient minds but still allows time for the reflection we need.

But what if it is not the right pace for you? No problem, but I would suggest you still give yourself a framework. For instance, you can decide to do a chapter every fortnight.

TAKE NOTES

It's a good idea to take notes as you read along. You can use a good old notebook or, even better, download the workbook I've created for you. There is space for notes alongside the trackers and exercises. You can print it out or use a PDF annotation app, like PDFelement or PDFescape.

If you're reading the eBook version, you can take notes within your Kindle app or device. Just long-press on text, and an icon with pen and paper will appear.

ASSESSMENTS

You'll find assessments throughout this book. You will want to write your answer down, whether in the book, your notebook, or the downloaded workbook, as you will want to refer to it later.

The idea is not to get to 0, but if you're at 30 (actual problem) and after implementing tools, you're at 20 (manageable problem), that's a win!

QUICK WINS VS LONG-TERM STRATEGIES

This book shares both quick wins and long-term strategies. Now, it is not always clear-cut what is what. Long-term strategies tend to take a bit more time, energy, or money to implement, or they can take longer to yield results.

Pick between 1-3 quick wins and 1 long-term strategy per week. I know your kind, you're going to be tempted to go all in and try everything until you're discouraged and don't want to try any. But this time, I'm asking you to put your imaginary lab coat on and pretend you are both the scientist and the guinea pig. And you can't adequately test effectiveness when there are too many components. So, in an ideal world, you pick 1-3, evaluate, keep, or drop, then pick another one. That's what the workbook is for. Speaking of which...

RESOURCES

At the end of the book you will find all the books, apps, and websites recommended here.

WORKBOOK

That's where the magic happens. Beside a space to take notes, fill out the assessments, and answer the reflection questions, you'll find a weekly task list that will help you track the tools you're picking up and evaluate them.

You can download it right here: bit.ly/adhdpowerup

BEFORE YOU START

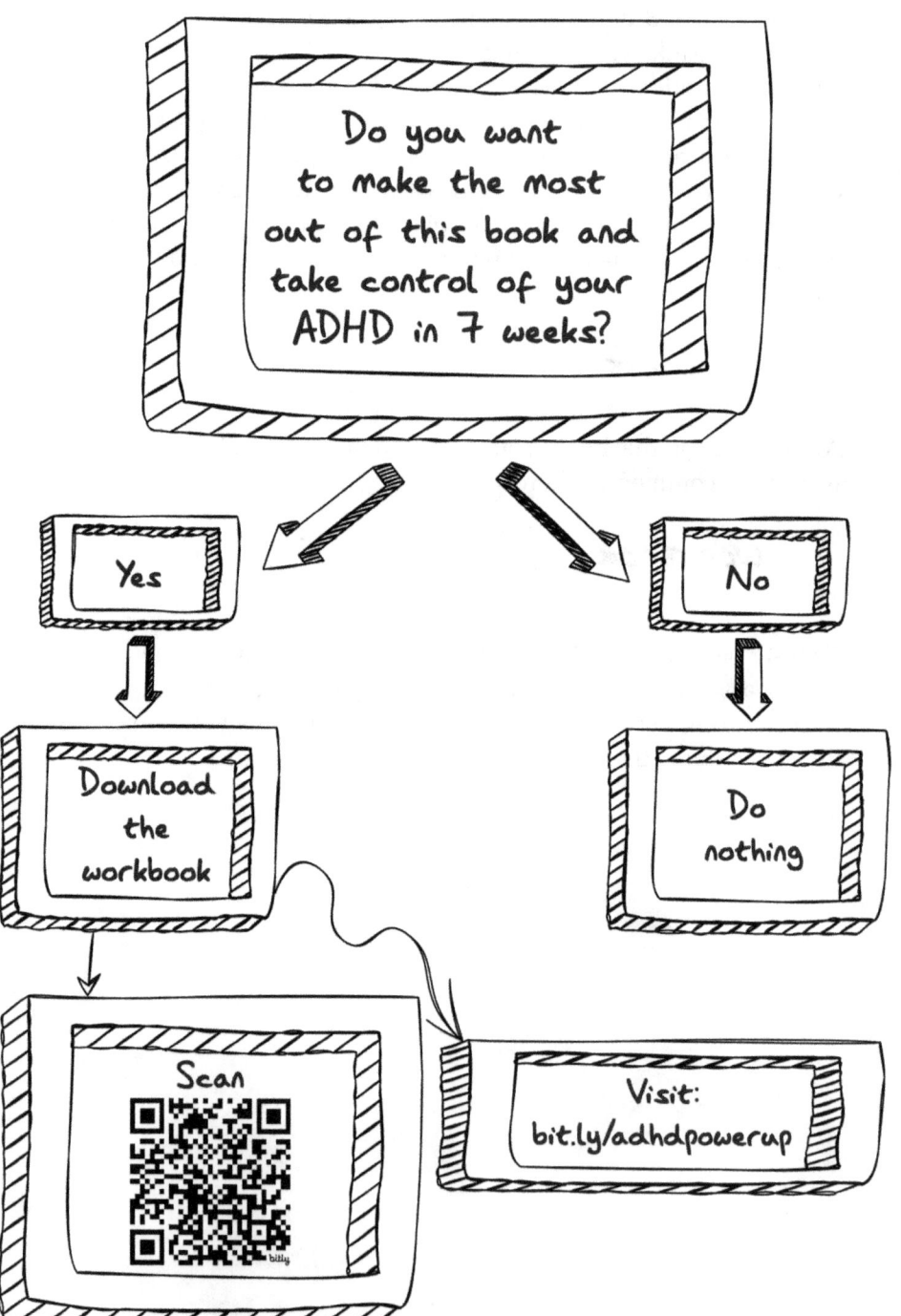

week 1: adhd, executive function, and you
MAPPING THE JOURNEY AHEAD

If you've picked up this book, you probably have a good idea of what ADHD is, and you want to know more about executive function and, more importantly, about executive dysfunction and what to do about it. Well, my friend, you've come to the right place! Before we move on to what to do, we need to take a moment to look into more details at executive function and its part in ADHD.

> But I don't want a lecture, Estelle, I want practical tools!

> I hear you, but knowledge is power, and a deeper understanding of what goes on in our neurospicy brains can help address the right problems and pick up the right tools.

1. EXECUTIVE DYSFUNCTION AND ADHD

Executive function is the film director of our lives: they have the overall vision, they know what the end goal is and what it should look like. They're involved at every stage, making all the big decisions but also supervising the organization, sequencing, and editing our thoughts and actions to make sure we achieve our goals on time.

Put in a more neurological way, executive function boils down to three main components:

1. **Working Memory** - Our ability to hold and manipulate information for a short amount of time, like remembering what your friends want to drink when ordering at the bar or why you're in the kitchen.
2. **Cognitive Flexibility** - Our ability to switch between tasks, adapt to change and challenges, take multiple perspectives, and adapt our beliefs in the light of new evidence.
3. **Inhibitory Control** - Our ability to control impulses and focus on a task while filtering distraction. That means even when your phone pings, you keep writing!

Does it sound like the trailer of an ADHD core symptoms movie you've seen before? Just you wait, the camera is still slightly out of focus on how it actually translates into our daily lives. So let's check the storyboard of our biopic.

Memory

Poor working memory is where we earn that "goldfish" label. You know, the one—where you can't seem to hold onto step-by-step instructions, lose your train of thought mid-conversation, or constantly misplace your keys because you can't remember where you put them.

Paired with poor inhibitory control, we lose track of the task at hand and forget what we were originally doing. Have you ever boiled the kettle and forgot to make tea? Have you ever started the laundry and left wet clothes in the washing machine for hours, if not days? Yes, me too.

Cognitive Flexibility

We've already touched on how tough it can be to switch from one task to another, especially when plans change unexpectedly. But poor cognitive flexibility can be sneakier than that. It can make taking feedback or criticism feel like the world is collapsing under our feet.

What others see as stubbornness is often our struggle to see multiple viewpoints. This rigidity doesn't just make transitions difficult; it can also cause friction in social interactions. Misunderstandings, paired with emotional rigidity, can make even the simplest conversation feel like navigating a minefield. But more on emotions later.

Organization

Messy, scattered, slob, clot, or whatever you've been called, it's not a character flaw; it's an executive function impairment!

The messy house, the lost keys, the piles of papers, the shoe box full of receipts… sounds familiar? Ever forgotten to pay the bills? Missed filing your taxes on time? Did you leave your laptop at home when you needed it for an important presentation? Yep, I thought so. Don't worry, we'll have a whole week dedicated to mastering space.

Time Management

Ah, time management—the poster child of ADHD struggles. Forgetting appointments, double-booking ourselves, being chronically late, not following schedule, inconsistent routine, or failure to meet deadlines—these are the visible symptoms. The real beast beneath the surface is time blindness.

Time blindness can have a devastating impact on our lives, with ramifications that extend way beyond a missed deadline or an unpaid bill. By leaving things to the last minute, underestimating the amount of time we need, over-committing, and neglecting the personal downtime we desperately need, our stress level can skyrocket, kicking off a whole new round of ADHD symptoms.

Productivity

You've probably guessed by now that all the executive function challenges mentioned directly impact productivity. But there's more.

When poor inhibitory control lets distractions in, working memory and cognitive flexibility team up to make task initiation feel like climbing Mount Everest. We struggle to plan, break down goals into manageable steps, prioritize, and then—when we finally have a plan—switching from planning mode to doing mode can feel impossible.

This mental strain leaves us frazzled and fatigued, which only sets off a vicious cycle of executive dysfunction. No wonder productivity feels like a distant dream.

Impulsivity

Let's get one thing clear: impulsivity is more than just buying something you don't need or blurting out an answer before thinking it through. Sure, these are worth addressing, and we will on week 6. But impulsivity touches so much more.

It's the reason we struggle with time management and organization. It can also lead to various serious issues, such as overeating, substance abuse, reckless driving, and other risky behaviors. Not to mention, impulsivity often leads to emotional outbursts. Speaking of outbursts, let's talk about emotions…

Emotional Dysregulation

Emotional regulation is like a three-legged stool, supported by all the main components of executive function.

Strong inhibitory control would allow us to hold back those knee-jerk reactions—the kind that isn't exactly socially acceptable or that we regret two minutes later. A healthy working memory would help us remember how similar situations turned out in the past, giving us some much-needed perspective. And cognitive flexibility? That's the magic that lets us see things from different angles, helping us shift our emotional response when needed and consider alternative explanations for what's triggering us. When all three work together, emotional regulation becomes much more manageable. But when they're out of whack—well, you know how that story goes.

Do you want to check what your personal challenges look like and where the need for improvement is? Go through the assessment below:

-> Assessment: Executive Function Skills Assessment

Instructions: *For each statement below, please rate the frequency with which you experience these situations using the following scale:*

0 = Never
1 = Rarely (once a month)
2 = Sometimes (once a week)
3 = Often (several times a week)
4 = Always (daily)

Memory

- *I forget to complete tasks I started, such as leaving laundry in the washing machine.*
- *I lose track of what I am doing when interrupted by another task or distraction.*
- *I struggle to retain step-by-step instructions soon after I hear them.*

Cognitive Flexibility

- *I find it difficult to adjust to sudden changes in plans or routines.*
- *I have trouble handling feedback or criticism without feeling defensive.*
- *I struggle to see situations from multiple perspectives, affecting my social interactions.*

Organization

- My personal and workspaces are often disorganized.
- I frequently misplace essential items like keys, wallets, or documents.
- I tend to forget deadlines or important commitments such as paying bills or work deadlines.

Time Management

- I often forget appointments or find myself double-booked.
- I am regularly late for meetings, work, or social engagements.
- I underestimate the time needed for tasks, leading to last-minute rushes.

Productivity

- I find initiating tasks overwhelming, especially planning and prioritizing steps.
- Distractions frequently disrupt my focus, impacting task completion.
- I feel mentally exhausted by the effort needed to stay on task.

Impulsivity

- I tend to make quick decisions or purchases without thorough consideration.
- I engage in risky behaviors more often than I feel is safe or appropriate.
- My emotional responses are often immediate and intense, sometimes leading to regrettable actions.

Emotional Dysregulation

- I react strongly to situations without thinking through the consequences.
- I find it hard to recall how I've successfully managed similar emotional situations in the past.
- It's difficult for me to adapt my emotional responses based on the context or feedback.

Scoring:

0-21: You may experience occasional challenges in executive functions.
22-42: Executive function challenges regularly impact your daily functioning.
43-63: You face significant difficulties in multiple areas of executive function that frequently impact your daily life.
64-84: Your executive function challenges consistently impair your functioning across most areas.

Over our seven weeks together, we will address each of those symptoms with quick wins and long-term strategies that will bear fruit for years to come. But before we jump in, let's examine the nuts and bolts of our brain a little further and examine the 'why.' Why is our executive function impaired?

2. WHY DOES ADHD AFFECT EXECUTIVE FUNCTION?

Biological Basics

If you've done any research on ADHD—or read my other books—you've probably come across the infamous duo: norepinephrine and dopamine. These neurotransmitters, when out of balance, are often blamed for our ADHD symptoms. However, when it comes to executive function, there are two other key players in the brain we need to talk about: the prefrontal cortex and basal ganglia.

Prefrontal Cortex

Think of the prefrontal cortex as the producer of our brain—it's the one making decisions, keeping us on track, and solving problems when things go wrong. Located just behind our forehead, it manages thoughts, actions, and emotions to help us reach our goals. Sounds like a pretty important gig, right? Well, for people with ADHD, it doesn't always run smoothly.

The 2018 Salavert study published in the *Journal of Attention Disorders* showed that adults with ADHD have trouble deactivating the

Default Mode Network (DMN)—the part of the brain responsible for daydreaming—when we need to focus. So, while we're trying to get things done, our DMN is still active, hogging the spotlight from the *Task-Positive Network* (TPN), which should be helping us pay attention.

In short, our brains don't always switch off the daydream mode when they're supposed to, making focus that much harder.

Basal Ganglia

Now, every producer needs a good assistant to keep things running smoothly, and that's where the basal ganglia come in. This group of structures fine-tunes movement, helps with decision-making, and regulates motivation. Think of it as the brain's First Assistant Director (1st AD), keeping everything on schedule and adapting when things go off course.

According to a 2021 study by Wang, there's evidence that the basal ganglia in people with ADHD mature more slowly, which contributes to symptoms like impulsivity and hyperactivity.

> Another lecture on neurology, Estelle! Yawn, babe.

> I know! But while ADHD's biological roots are complex, I'm telling you all this because understanding how our brains work—or don't—can help us make sense of our struggles.

The Stress Feedback Loop

Let's not get into the nature/nurture debate surrounding ADHD. Whether you think ADHD is purely biological or environmental, or you sit somewhere in between with the biosocial model: we don't exist in a vacuum. So, for better or worse, external factors have an influence. For better is picking up a book to find strategies, for instance (hint, hint), and for worse, in this case, is stress.

Comb's 2015 study on the relationship between stress and ADHD symptoms found a significant connection. Looking at 983 participants, the researchers found that we're more sensitive to stress due to our cognitive symptoms, and in turn, stress makes those symptoms worse—creating a vicious cycle. We get stressed, our symptoms get worse, we get more stressed, our symptoms get even worse, etc. You get the idea.

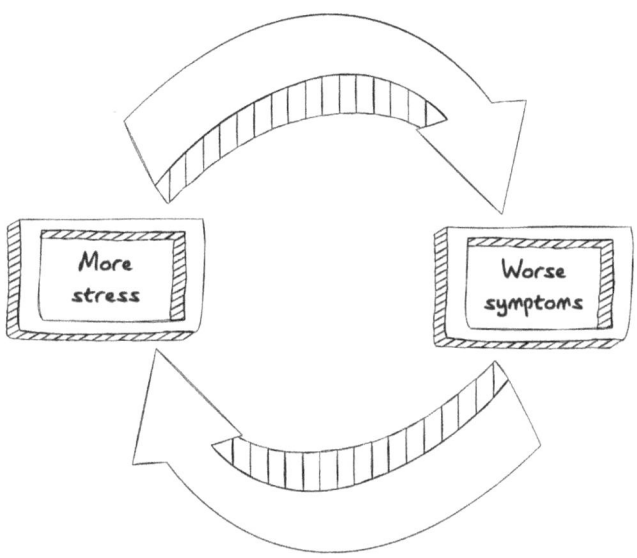

Another 2015 study published in the journal *Psychoneuroendocrinology* also examined stress and suggested that our HPA axis, a system that regulates our stress response, works differently for us and affects our cortisol level, a stress hormone, potentially leading to chronic stress. But wait—it gets worse!

A few years later, in 2021, some researchers from the Institute for Forensic Psychology and Psychiatry at Saarland University, Germany, looked at 230 adults with ADHD and how they dealt with stress. They found that the ADHD group often opted for "maladaptive coping strategies (avoidance, escape, social withdrawal, rumination, resignation, self-pity, self-blame, aggression, and drug use)." They concluded that "some maladaptive coping strategies increased current life impairments over and above the effects of ADHD and further psychological distress." Okay, so bluntly put, we perceive higher levels of stress than neurotypical people, and we're not good at coping with it, as we don't apply helpful strategies.

The good news? Coping strategies can be learned! That's why having a personalized toolkit for managing stress is key—and we're about to build yours.

3. A NEW HOPE

After what I just wrote, you might be feeling deflated. I mean, if it is biological and given the stressful world we live in, we might as well give up, right? Absolutely not! Not on my watch. "The only way is up, baby!" as Yazz would have said in 1988.

If you've picked this book, you're determined to improve your executive function, and so should you! Because, friend, there is hope. And this hope has a name: let me introduce you to the neuroplasticity and mindset virtuous cycle, a superhero at your service to fight the villain stress and executive dysfunction vicious cycle.

Neuroplasticity-Mindset Virtuous Cycle

For those of us who get an ADHD diagnosis as adults, it can be a double-edged sword. On one hand, it's a relief to finally understand why we've struggled. On the other hand, it can leave us feeling like we're stuck in a cycle of failure, and the biological explanation makes it a fatality. But that's forgetting about the power of neuroplasticity.

Neuroplasticity is the brain's remarkable ability to reorganize and form new connections, no matter your age or whether you have ADHD. Since the 1970s, research—starting with Dr. Michael Merzenich—has shown that our brains can adapt and change, even when we face challenges. Today, it is a well-established concept and is used both in therapy and medication to help manage symptoms of ADHD and improve cognitive function.

On the other hand, a growth mindset, a concept developed by Carol Dweck, is the idea that abilities can be developed by learning and a bit of effort, unlike a fixed mindset, where we feel stuck.

A 2020 study published in the *Journal of Social and Clinical Psychology* found that people with ADHD who embraced a growth mindset had better self-regulation and coping skills.

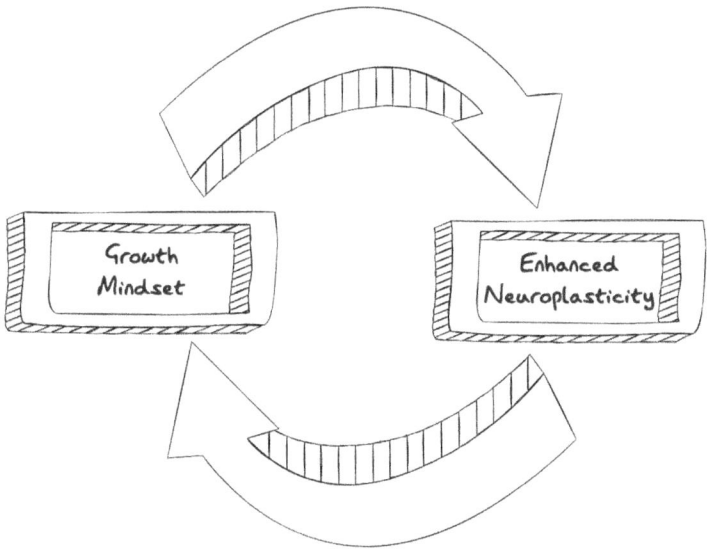

So, want to strengthen that growth mindset on your executive function journey? You should. It's well worth it. Here are 10 strategies to get you started:

1. **Embrace Imperfections** - Acknowledge your flaws without judgment—progress starts here.
2. **Embrace Challenges** - Step out of your comfort zone and reframe challenges as learning opportunities.
3. **Scrap "Failing" and Adopt "Learning"** - So you messed up? Start asking: how can I improve the plan, the goal, or the process next time?
4. **Stop Comparing** - Life is not a race, and more specifically, it is not a competition.
5. **See the Big Picture** - Cultivate a sense of purpose beyond yourself and what you aim to achieve in the long term.
6. **Enjoy the Journey** - Celebrate progress, not just the end goal.
7. **Use "Yet"** - Add "yet" to your can't-do list. "I can't stick to a schedule... yet!"

8. **Reverse Engineer** - Rather than getting envious, be curious about how others succeed and learn from it.
9. **Daily Reflection** - Reflect on what's working and what's not.
10. **Invite Constructive Feedback** - Learn to accept constructive criticism as a tool for growth.

Throughout this book, you will have opportunities to develop your growth mindset. Just keep in mind that this is not an overnight transformation.

-> *Reflect:*

At the moment, how do I view and talk about ADHD and executive function? Do I use words like "suffer from" or "afflicted by"?

A HOLISTIC APPROACH

I don't mean 'holistic' in a 'using crystals and burning sage' way. However, if that helps you, I'm right behind you. I'm talking about encompassing the whole person. Let's imagine for a moment that you have broken a leg.

> You said there is hope, Estelle, and now you want to give me a broken leg too!

> It's just a metaphor. Bare with me for a minute.

Let's rewind. You were happily cycling along the coast, daydreaming away. You didn't see that rock on the ground; the impact sent you off flying, and in an incomprehensible prowess you didn't even know you had, you somersaulted into the air to try and land back on your feet. But then, ouch, that was too much force on one leg. Fast forward through the ambulance trip and the wait in the Accidents and Emergency department; the doctor tells you, you have broken your leg and sends you home with... not a band-aid... but only a pair of crutches.

> Wait, what? Just a pair of crutches? No cast, no boot, no painkiller?

> Yep, just crutches.

That's basically what happens when a well-meaning person tells you to follow their routine to boost your executive function. With a broken leg and just crutches, my guess is that you will be able to go about, but you will be in pain, and more importantly, your broken bone is going to take longer to heal and will probably fuse in a misaligned way creating a lifelong limp. With a cast on, the external support allows the internal repair to happen.

Now, don't get me wrong—you are not broken! But for long-lasting executive function improvement, you can't rely on external support alone. The work has to take place both from the outside in and from the inside out. Through these seven weeks, I will present you with a range of tools and techniques that will offer external support while taking you through the internal transformation that will empower you to finally create habits that stick without the burnout.

So, you've already done the 'diagnosis' earlier in this chapter. Now, let's start planning the 'treatment.'

4. EXECUTIVE FUNCTION AUDIT

We've established that executive dysfunction is at the core of ADHD symptoms, but it's not the only factor that can impact how our brains function. You are more than your ADHD, and it's essential to take a multi-directional approach.

Is it ADHD?

First, if you're a woman and you're getting to a certain age, you want to look into the impact of menopause on executive function, as it can affect memory and concentration, cognitive processing speed, decision-making, multitasking, mood, and anxiety. And that's for any woman! For us with ADHD, Wasserstein's 2023 study found the impact of hormonal changes during menopause and perimenopause worsens ADHD symptoms, such as inattention, disorganization, poor time management, emotional dysregulation, procrastination, impulsivity, and brain fog.

If you're interested in the specific experience of ADHD for women, I cover late diagnosis and the impact of hormones on our symptoms in my *Empowering Books for Women with ADHD*. Other hormonal changes associated with puberty, pregnancy, and postpartum can also affect executive function. Managing your hormones, as well as your ADHD, could greatly benefit your executive function.

Neurological disorders can also impair executive function: traumatic brain injuries, of course, but also stroke, Alzheimer's disease and other dementias, Parkinson's disease, and Multiple Sclerosis (MS). So, while some memory degradation is normal with aging, ADHD or not, if your executive dysfunction has suddenly worsened, it's worth consulting a doctor to rule out other issues.

Besides ADHD, other mental health conditions and developmental disorders can affect executive function. Special mention to depression, anxiety disorders, and learning disabilities like dyslexia, which are classic ADHD comorbidities. And let's not forget that Bipolar Disorder and Autism Spectrum Disorder (ASD) can similarly affect executive function.

Lifestyle and Executive Function

Stress has already been mentioned, but other environmental and lifestyle factors, such as sleep quality, nutrition, exercise, alcohol, and substance abuse, can also impact executive function. To evaluate the impact of your environment and lifestyle on your executive function, take the following assessment.

-> Assessment: Lifestyle Impact on Executive Function

Instructions: For each statement below, please rate the frequency with which you experience these situations using the following scale:

0 = Never
1 = Rarely (less than once a month)
2 = Sometimes (once a week)
3 = Often (several times a week)
4 = Always (daily)

- How often do you feel rested after a night's sleep?
- How often do you eat whole foods like fruits, vegetables, and whole grains instead of processed foods and snacks?
- How often do you engage in at least 30 minutes of moderate physical activity?
- How often do you participate in activities that require active learning or problem-solving?
- How often do you feel calm in your home environment?
- How often do you feel supported by your work or school environment in managing your ADHD symptoms?
- How often do you engage in social activities that you find enjoyable and fulfilling?
- How often do you use effective strategies such as meditation, therapy, or physical activity to manage stress?
- How often do you refrain from or avoid consuming alcohol and substances that can affect your mood and energy levels?
- How often do you switch off digital devices to avoid sleep disturbances or procrastination?

Scoring:

31-40: Lifestyle and environmental factors have little to no impact on your executive function.
21-30: Some lifestyle and environmental factors occasionally affect your executive function.
11-20: Several lifestyle and environmental factors frequently impact your executive function.
0-10: Lifestyle and environmental factors regularly and negatively impact your executive function.

Now, there are times when life just happens, and we go through a stressful time with no or little control. Besides the hormonal impact, becoming a parent can affect executive function due to lack of sleep, increased demands on cognitive resources such as multi-tasking and decision-making, and increased responsibilities and stress.

Other significant life changes, such as grief, or less dramatic ones, such as a career change or moving house, can all put pressure on our executive function. It's essential to be aware of those changes and remember that they will evolve and that an adequate coping mechanisms toolkit will help navigate complicated times.

STARTING BLOCKS

As a starting point for our seven-week journey together, you need to assess where you're starting from and where you want to go. By going through the following reflections, you will set realistic goals and create your personalized plan for the next six weeks.

-> *Reflect: Program Audit*

1. Time and Effort Commitment

- *How many hours per week are you realistically able to commit to this program? (Please consider your other obligations like work, family, and leisure.) Block the time down in your diary for the next 6 weeks.*
- *On a scale of 1 to 10, how much effort are you willing to invest in this program? (1 being the least effort, and 10 being the maximum effort.)*

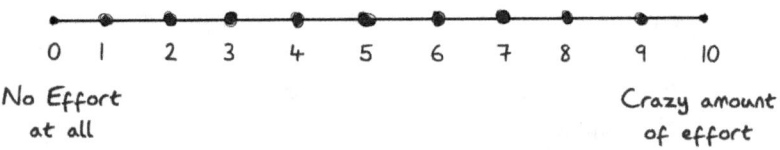

2. Priority

- *Refer back to the Executive Function Skills Assessment at the beginning of this chapter and break down your score for each section.*
- *Which ones are the highest? Is it memory, productivity, or emotional regulation?*
- *Please rank the following areas in order of priority for you (1 being the highest priority):*

- *Memory*
- *Cognitive Flexibility*
- *Organization*
- *Time Management*
- *Productivity*
- *Impulsivity*
- *Emotional Dysregulation*

- *What are your three priorities?*
- *What is your top priority?*

3. Goals and Expectations

- *What specific changes do you hope to see in your daily life as a result of improving these skills? E.g., "I hope to stay focused on tasks without getting distracted.*
- *Why does this goal matter? E.g., "Because I feel stuck in my career, and I know I can do better."*
- *On a scale from 1 to 10, how able are you to do this at the moment?*

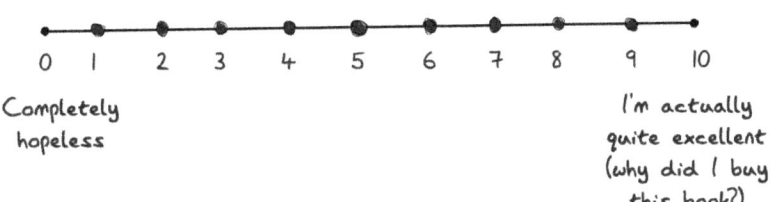

- *What would you like to be able to do better by the end of this program? For example, "I want to be able to express my emotions more constructively."*

- *Why does this goal matter? For example, "Because it's taking a toll on my relationship with my partner, and I'm emotionally tired."*
- *On a scale from 1 to 10, how able are you to do this at the moment?*

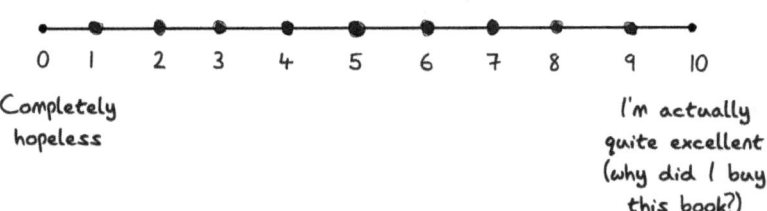

0 — Completely hopeless

9 — I'm actually quite excellent (why did I buy this book?)

4. Challenges

What challenges do you anticipate in sticking to your goals? What is going to go wrong?

What tools and strategies do you already know and can put in place to help you stick to your goal? (E.g., reminders, accountability partner). If you can't think of anything, don't worry, we will address it during the program.

FINAL THOUGHTS

> Okay, but where are the tools, Estelle?

> Don't worry, they're coming!

But before diving into the 'how,' we needed to shine a light on the 'why.' Because understanding what's really happening in those neurospicy brains of ours is going to help us address the right problems with the right solutions.

This week, we've mapped out the big picture, and it was all about laying the groundwork—understanding what executive function is and how it plays out in your life. And those challenges? They're not a life sentence. You can improve them. And not just by throwing productivity hacks and hoping for the best. We will take a deeper, more holistic approach—one that works from the outside in and the inside out.

Now that we've got a clearer picture, we're ready to get to the good stuff. Over the next six weeks, we'll start building your personalized toolkit—packed with practical tools, mindset shifts, and strategies that work for your ADHD brain. So take a breath and give yourself some credit for making it through this first chapter; it was a hefty one. You also reflected on where you feel the most challenged, and that's a brave move. Now, time to roll up our sleeves and start building that executive function toolkit—together!

KEY TAKEAWAYS

- **Executive dysfunction** is at the heart of ADHD symptoms, making everything from staying organized to managing time feel like an uphill battle.
- **Working memory, cognitive flexibility, and inhibitory control** are the three main pillars of executive function—and when they're not working well, life gets messy (literally and figuratively).
- **Main struggles include** memory issues, cognitive flexibility, time management, organization, productivity, impulsivity, and emotional regulation.
- **Stress and ADHD** create a vicious cycle. Stress makes our symptoms worse, and those worsened symptoms cause even more stress. Breaking the cycle is key.
- **Neuroplasticity and a growth mindset** create a virtuous cycle. Our brains can rewire and improve at any age, giving us hope for real, lasting change in our executive function. A growth mindset is about learning, adapting, and celebrating progress—even the small wins!

week 2: train your brain

SHARPEN MEMORY, FOCUS AND ATTENTION

NOW THAT WE know about our prefrontal cortex, the Default Mode Network not switching off, and the basal ganglia not maturing, here comes the moment you've all been waiting for... drum roll... the answers to "what can we do about it" and emerge out of the fog. But just before that, let's assess where we're starting from.

> What? But I've just done an assessment, Estelle!

> I know, I know. But it was a general one. This one is specifically for memory and attention

-> Assessment: Working Memory and Inattention

Instructions: *For each statement below, please rate the frequency with which you experience these situations using the following scale:*

0 = Never
1 = Rarely (less than once a month)

2 = *Sometimes (once a week)*
3 = *Often (several times a week)*
4 = *Always (daily)*

Working Memory

- **Forgetting Names or Appointments**: *How often do you forget names, appointments, or important dates?*
- **Task Instructions**: *How often do you ask for instructions again on something you were just told?*
- **Multi-step Tasks**: *How often do you fail to complete tasks that require remembering a sequence of steps?*
- **Daily Necessities**: *How often do you forget why you entered a room or what you were about to do?*
- **Conversational Details**: *How often have you forgotten details of a conversation shortly after it took place?*

Inattention

- **Focusing on Tasks**: *How often do you find yourself unable to stay focused on tasks or activities, both at work and at home?*
- **Listening in Conversations**: *How often do you catch yourself not listening when someone is speaking to you directly?*
- **Completion of Projects**: *How often do you leave projects unfinished, not due to lack of interest but due to inattention?*
- **Attention to Detail in Work**: *How often do you make errors in tasks that require attention to detail?*
- **Ignoring Instructions**: *How often do you miss out on important instructions or details because you are not paying attention?*

Scoring

0-10: *There are very few occasions where working memory or attention issues affect daily functioning.*
11-20: *There are occasional difficulties with memory and attention, slightly affecting daily activities.*
21-30: *Working memory and attention issues are regularly observed and clearly impact daily activities.*
31-40: *There are daily challenges with memory and attention, significantly affecting performance and productivity.*

1. REFOCUSING FROM THE OUTSIDE IN

When trying to improve working memory and attention, there are a few lifestyle strategies we can implement that can have a positive impact very quickly. To caricaturize, if you're not sleeping, drinking alcohol or using other substances most days, and eating junk while stressing about what you haven't done and should be doing, that's not going to help your brain. So, what can?

GOOD SLEEP

First things first. Are you getting enough sleep? The American Academy of Sleep Medicine (AASM) and the Sleep Research Society (SRS) developed a consensus recommendation of at least 7 hours of sleep per night for optimal health. A recent study in *Frontiers in Human Neuroscience* suggested that sleep deprivation disrupts connectivity between our old friend the default mode network (DMN), and other critical brain networks.

Where it gets even trickier for us is that the same DMN not switching off might well be one of the reasons we're struggling to switch off and fall asleep in the first place. Our Dopamine and Noradrenaline imbalance is also to blame, as well as a possible delayed Circadian Rhythm, a.k.a. our body clock. If you're having trouble falling asleep or staying asleep, finding strategies to help you clock your 7 hours could make a huge improvement to your working memory and executive function in general, as soon as one good night's sleep.

-> Quick Wins: 7 Tricks to Promote Sleep

1. **Consistency**: Pick a bedtime and a wake-up time and stick to it even on weekends.
2. **Embrace Goldilocks**: Is it too hot, too cold, too bright, or too itchy? Help your circadian rhythm with black-out curtains or a natural light alarm. Make sure your bed is 'just right,' not too firm, not too soft, with comfortable pillows and soft sheets.

3. **Get Comfortable**: if you can't modify your environment, try a sleeping mask or earplugs. Make sure you wear what is comfortable for you, don't hesitate to experiment. Try wearing socks to help regulate your body temperature.
4. **Switch off stimulants**: Avoid coffee and other stimulants at least 6 hours before bedtime.
5. **Evening Wind-Down**: If you've read *The Empowering ADHD Workbook for Women,* you know all about crafting a calming bedtime routine. If you haven't yet, try preparing for tomorrow today, journaling, reading, and relaxing.
6. **Switch off**: Turn off electronic devices at least one hour before bed to reduce blue light exposure and stimulation.
7. **Listen up**: Listen to white noise, guided meditation, or relaxing sounds. The app *InsightTimer* offers many free and paid options. You could also try the progressive muscle relaxation technique.

If all fails, you had a bad night and you can't thread two thoughts together during the day, try Yoga Nidra. This is my secret weapon for when fatigue gets through the roof. Don't be misled by the word "yoga," it doesn't involve exercise and it can be shorter and more efficient than a nap. In fact it doesn't involve moving at all: it is a form of body scan that takes you into a deep form of relaxation without falling asleep. Try it now, thank me later.

Nourish Your Brain

Food can have a huge impact on our executive function, as I've already shared in *Brain Boosting Food for Women with ADHD,* adopting an 'ADHD diet' has had the fastest and most noticeable impact on lifting my brain fog. Want the low down? Here you go.

-> Quick Wins: 10 Steps to Nourishing Your Brain

1. **Avoid processed food and sugar** that can disrupt serotonin production and exacerbate ADHD symptoms, particularly mood swings.

2. **Try an elimination diet**: If you think you might have a food intolerance, simply remove the ingredient entirely for a month, then eat it with nothing else. Take notes before and after and notice any changes.
3. **Check you're getting enough protein** (depending on your age, gender, etc.) and make sure to spread them throughout the day.
4. **Boost your healthy fat intake** by introducing nuts, seeds, and fatty fish to your diet.
5. **Swap processed for wholegrain** when it comes to rice, bread, and pasta. They have more protein and more fiber, which helps stabilize blood sugar.
6. **Eat the rainbow** for more fiber and all the vitamins you can get.
7. **Hydrate!** Dehydration can seriously impact brain function, so make sure you're getting enough water, whatever it takes. Keep a water bottle on your desk, add fresh fruits or herbs, or track it on a planner or an app like *My Hydration* or *Drink Water*.
8. **Check your stimulants:** Make sure you're not drinking too much coffee or other caffeinated drinks. The recommended maximum intake is 400mg, which is about 5 cups.
9. **Be mindful of your alcohol consumption**, not for moral reasons but because of its effect on brain function, and Substance Abuse Disorder can be an ADHD comorbidity. If you have any doubts, take the Alcohol Use Disorders Identification Test (AUDIT). The link is in the resources.
10. **Document** changes you implement to check their efficacy and review regularly.

Move It

I know, I know—you've probably heard it a thousand times: exercise is good for you, and it helps with ADHD symptoms. But hear me out, there's a reason why this advice keeps coming up.

Take this 2019 study from *Frontiers in Psychiatry*, researchers looked at MRI scans of 23 adults with ADHD after just 30 minutes of exercise compared to after watching a movie. The results? A single session of aerobic exercise, like biking, significantly boosted executive function—especially in attention and decision-making. And if that's not enough to get you reaching out for your sneakers, a 2023 study in *Frontiers in Molecular Neuroscience* showed that exercise also enhances neuroplasticity.

Okay, are you convinced by now that we've got to "move it, move it," even if we don't like it? And in this case, I'm not talking about Reel 2 Real. No, getting "physically fit" or "sweet" has nothing to do with it.

Now, what can you do if, like me, the idea of sweating in lycra in a spinning class is as appealing as walking through fire? You can make it fun. Here are 25 creative and fun aerobic exercises that might make the experience more enjoyable. Have a look at those ideas and try one if you think you could benefit from more movement in your life.

-> Quick Wins: 15 fun ways to move it

1. **Dance Classes**: There are just so many to choose from, from Salsa to Hip Hop, Zumba to Bollywood, line dancing to tap. Long gone are the days when you had to choose between Classical and Jazz.
2. **Video Games:** Like old school Wii Sports where you can box, sword fight, or row without leaving your living room.
3. **Hiking:** With the added benefits of being outdoors and improving your body clock.
4. **Group Sports** for the added socializing benefits. You can go for classics like basketball, or look further to lacrosse, beach volley or roller derby, for instance.
5. **Outdoor Cycling**: Just enjoy a trail without the pressure of a spin class.
6. **Outdoor Swimming**: With added health and well-being benefits from cold water swimming, or "blue therapy."
7. **Trampoline Jumping**: Channel the kid in you. Or go with your children if they can stand the embarrassment.
8. **Roller Skating or Rollerblading** either outdoors or at your local rink.

9. **Kayaking or Canoeing** for adventure and exercise if you have a lake, a river or the ocean near you.
10. **Power Walking**: Just go for a walk, but make it fast.
11. **Boxing or Kickboxing** to blow some steam off at the same time.
12. **Parkour**: To transform your city into a gym.
13. **Interactive Fitness Apps**: Do you need a reason to run? Try getting chased by zombies with an app like *Zombie, Run!*
14. **Skateboarding**: Whether to go places or hit your local skate park.
15. **Hula Hooping**: Do it solo or in a class.

2. REFOCUSING FROM THE INSIDE OUT

You remember neuroplasticity, right? In short, we can train our brains, and yes, even with ADHD. Does it happen overnight? No. Is it worth it? Let's try and find out.

Brain Aerobic

There are many ways we can train your brain to improve working memory and attention. You would have probably heard of doing crosswords or sudoku for older people to slow down memory loss. Well, guess what? That can be helpful for us, too. There is also specific training, backed by research, particularly suited for adults with ADHD.

Let me introduce you to Dual N-Back, a cognitive training tool designed to boost working memory and fluid intelligence—your ability to solve new problems without prior knowledge. Originally a psychological test from the 1950s, it's now widely used in cognitive research to improve attention and executive function, though there's still a debate about its impact on overall intelligence.

But does it work for us with ADHD? In short, yes. A 2020 study by Japanese and Swiss scientists had adults with ADHD do 30 minutes of Dual N-Back training for 20 days. Those who did the adaptive version (where tasks get harder as you improve) showed significant improvements in managing distractions, whether or not they were on medication.

Want to try it? Visit Brain Workshop, which offers a free, open-source version of the training for Windows, Mac, and Linux. Prefer an app on your phone? Try *N-Back*, which has a clean interface, various levels for that adaptive effect, and counts down rounds to keep you going.

The more you practice, the more the potential benefits. So this is a long-term strategy.

-> Long-term strategy: Dual N-Back Training Plan

- Train 5 times a week for about 25 minutes/day.
- Schedule when you're going to do it.
- Try pairing up with someone. It will help you stick with it. Or plan a reward for keeping at it for a month.
- Review your progress after 20 sessions (or about a month)

BRAIN CROSS TRAINING

Now, I get it: you might find that Dual N-Back training lacks variety. If you like the idea of a brain gym but want to cross-train, of course, there are tons of apps for that. You could try a communication-based app like *Elevate*, or pick *BrainHQ*, which works on improving attention, brain speed, memory, and navigation.

You could also choose to learn something new or play a strengthening brain game. There are plenty of online or offline options, depending on when and where you want to practice and whether you want the added benefits of socialization. All of the following are known to enhance working memory and attention:

- **Puzzle Building**: Jigsaws require sustained attention and visual memory skills.
- **Playing Cards**: Bridge, Poker, Memory, or any card game that requires you to track cards.
- **Reading and Summarizing**: Whether you join a book club or start a bookstagram account, summarizing aloud or in writing reinforces attention.

- **Play Chess**: Or another strategy game that requires critical thinking and sustained attention.
- **Learn a New Language**: As it will engage your memory.
- **Play Crosswords or Sudoku**: To challenge verbal and numeric memory

Now, just like the Dual N-Back exercise, you're not going to be able to measure working memory improvement after one game of chess. So, if you want to give brain cross-training a proper go, you need a training plan.

> -> *Long-term strategy: Brain Cross-Training Plan*

- Pick a brain training activity. You can check a few apps, or try a few different games for a couple of days, then pick the one that excites you the most.
- Schedule when you're going to practice. Ideally daily, or at least 5 times/week.
- Review your progress after 20 sessions (or about a month) and decide whether to continue, switch to another activity, or add another activity.

EVERYDAY ATHLETE

Are you feeling more like an everyday athlete, the one who runs after the bus and picks the stairs over the elevator but hates the gym? To train your brain with everyday tasks, you could try shopping without a shopping list, or remembering the names of all the people in your dance class by using a mnemonic, like the Memory Palace Technique (also known as the Method of Loci), where you associate a familiar setting with what you need to remember.

Let's pretend you're on your way back from work, your phone is dead, and you have nothing to write with. You know you have a full-on day tomorrow, and you want to buy ingredients to cook yourself a brain-boosting breakfast. You start to make a mental shopping list: eggs, smoked salmon, coffee… Now, you're worried you're not going to be able to remember all this, so you start creating a palace, in this case your home. You imagine the route from your front door to the fridge and visualize placing each grocery item at a 'landmark' on your route. So, you end up with a path that looks something like this:

1. I open the door, I leave it ajar by resting the coffee pack on the door frame.
2. I reach the shoe rack and carefully place one egg in each shoe, taking great care as I remove them from the egg box.
3. As I get to the living room, I hide the smoked salmon under the sofa pillow
4. I kick the jug of milk in the corridor, taking me to the kitchen
5. On the kitchen counter, I stab a multigrain loaf of bread repetitively, pretending to be in a Hitchcock movie.
6. On the kitchen table, I play boules with oranges.
7. As I finally open the fridge door, I see a tower of baked bean cans resembling an Andy Warhol painting.

There. As you can tell, the more fun you have with it, the more likely you are to remember it. Your shopping experience will never be the same again. Start small and increase the size of your list as your confidence grows.

-> Long-term strategy: Put Your Brain to Work

- Pick an everyday challenge to use your memory. Start small and with something with not too much consequence: names at the next party, a few items on your shopping list, etc.
- Review and assess how it went.
- Pick another challenge. Raise the bar if the first one went well: you could add a few items to your list or the number of names. Or keep a similar challenge if you struggled with the first one.
- Review and repeat.

EVERYDAY ATHLETE CHALLENGE

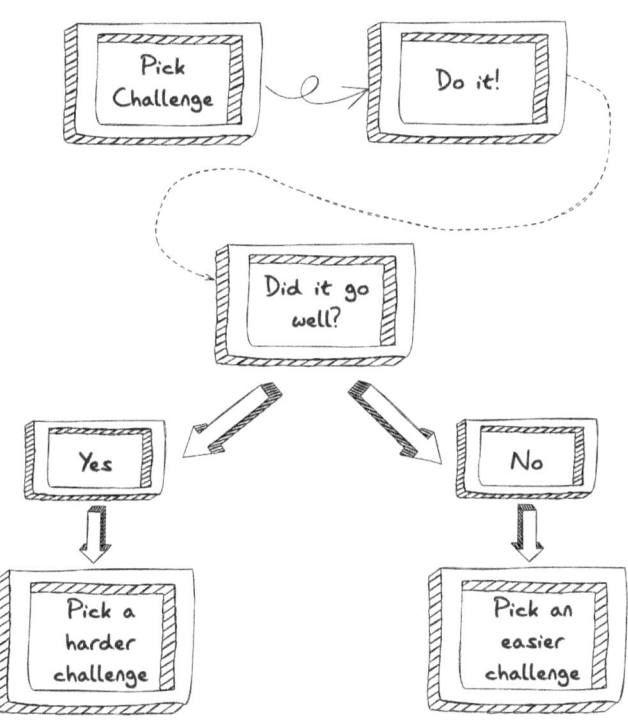

NEUROFEEDBACK THERAPY

Want to hear about a brain-training method that feels like sci-fi? Let's talk about Neurofeedback therapy. While it seems cutting-edge, it's actually been around since the 1920s, when scientists first recorded electrical activity in the brain. By the 60s, neurofeedback was being paired with conditioning techniques to help people control their brain activity. In the 70s and 80s, it was used to improve focus and reduce impulsivity in ADHD. With advances in computer tech, it's reached a whole new level today.

A 2014 meta-analysis by Holtmann concluded, "Neurofeedback has gained some promising empirical support." But a 2017 triple-blind study found it's not necessarily superior to cognitive-behavioral therapy. So, how does it work?

During a session, electrodes are placed on your scalp to monitor your brainwaves. You'll watch a movie or play a game, and when your focus drops, the screen pauses, prompting your brain to refocus. The effects are long-lasting, but it takes 20-40 sessions to see real benefits. It's also a financial investment, with costs starting around $150/month, plus equipment.

-> Long-term strategy: Finding the Right Neurofeedback Therapy

- Start by checking whether a referral from your healthcare provider is possible and whether the cost can be covered depending on your region and circumstances.
- If you can't get a referral, look at professional organizations such as The Biofeedback Certification International Alliance (BCIA) or The International Society for Neurofeedback & Research (ISNR) to see if there are any therapists near you.
- For cost or convenience, you might want to consider at-home options like *Myndlift* or *Neuroptimal*.
- Commit to at least 20 sessions, one to three times a week.

Now, imagine you're going to the gym every day, lifting weights, really focusing on a training program to build muscles, but then, on the other hand, you only eat junk food loaded with carbs and sugar. Is that going to get in the way of muscle building? I'm not a personal trainer, but I'd say: "Yes, big time, friend!" Well, guess what, similarly, all that exercising to pump our brain up is great, but if on the other end, we're up to our eyeballs in stress, all that time at the brain gym might be for nothing. So let's see how we can tune down stress and break that vicious cycle for good.

3. BREAKING THE CYCLE

Last week, we talked about the impact of stress on executive function and the feedback loops it creates for people with ADHD. Sadly, we can't turn off stress with the flick of a switch, but we can turn down the volume. Sure, there are external factors that might add to your stress, from Colin from accounting, who's at it to get you, to your toddler, who's refusing to get dressed when it's time for nursery, and don't mention the cost of living crisis, the climate emergency, and global politics! I hear you, and I have all of those too, minus the toddler who is now a tween, but let me tell you, that doesn't make it less stressful.

First, let's tease things out a bit. There is stress and stress. Actually, to be precise, there are three different types of stress:

1. There is **good stress** like a deadline that helps you get things done or stress before an interview that helps you perform better. Let's park good stress for future chapters.
2. There is also **getting stressed temporarily** when Colin messages you at 11 pm because you've left the lights on and he can see on the CCTV camera on his phone that you were last in the building. (Side note: in case you have any doubt, this is not acceptable behavior from Colin.)
3. And there is **living in a permanent state of stress**, regardless of what Colin or your toddler just did or didn't do, with a huge toll on mental health and impact on ADHD symptoms.

Let's be honest—living in a permanent state of calm isn't realistic. But what we can do is learn how to step out of that constant state of stress, focus on what we can control, and get better at bringing ourselves back to calm after a stressful moment.

And I've got some excellent news: the external strategies we've already discussed—healthy eating, proper sleep, and regular exercise—are at the top of the list for reducing stress. So you're already feeding two birds with one crumb. Now, what else can we do to lower stress and support working memory and attention?

Breath

Besides taking a deep breath when stress levels get too high, there are techniques you can practice regularly to regulate your stress hormones and increase your oxygen supply which will sharpen focus. There are many out there to choose from and if you really want to nerd down on breath work, you could look for specific classes in your region. In the meantime, I've selected three exercises that are particularly helpful both for stress and memory.

1. **Box Breathing**: I love the simplicity of box breathing, which is known to increase concentration. Breathe in through the nose for a count of 4, hold for 4, exhale through your mouth for a count of 4, hold your empty breath for and 4, repeat.
2. **4-7-8 Breathing**: This exercise also focuses on counting breaths and has been specifically devised to regulate the nervous system and improve focus. Breathe through the nose for 4, hold your breath for 7, exhale forcefully for 8 while making a "whoosh" sound with your mouth.
3. **Alternate Nostril Breathing**: This technique is known to balance both hemispheres of the brain, which helps calm the mind and promotes clearer thinking. Close your right nostril with your right thumb and inhale with your left nostril. Then close your left nostril with your ring finger while freeing your right nostril and exhale through your right nostril. Inhale through the right nostril, close it, open the left nostril, and exhale through it. Inhale through the left nostril, close it, open the right nostril, and exhale through it, etc. End your session with an exhale on the left side.

Now, most people will tell you that the benefits of breathwork come from regular practice over time (and they're right), but it's even better: a 2022 study published in *Frontiers in Psychology* found that participants were more accurate on the n-back task *right after* a slow yoga breathing session—including alternate nostril breathing. So, while practicing regularly will definitely pay off, you can still score a quick win by sneaking in a short breathwork session before diving into a task that needs your full attention. Think of it as a little mental warm-up!

-> *Quick win: Breathwork*

- Pick the breathing exercise the most appealing to you.
- Decide when you're going to practice it. Think about when

it would be most valuable, for instance before work, or after lunch.
- Decide where you're going to do it. Consider simplicity and privacy.
- Set up a reminder to get into the habit.
- Record any changes or improvements you notice.

MEDITATION

I'm fully aware that it might not be what you want to hear, but meditation has been extensively studied for its positive effects on executive function and is very high on the list of tools that can improve executive function, including attention, as well as relieve stress. It can benefit a whole range of ADHD symptoms and I could have fitted it in any other week of this program. Is it good for productivity? Check! Is it good to master time? Check! Does it help with impulsivity and emotional regulation? You bet! But the reason I wanted to include it in week 2, is because it is a foundational aspect of ADHD management.

It's not me saying it, Sumantry's 2021 meta-analysis suggests "that generalized attention, its alerting and executive control networks, and the inhibition and updating facets of executive control are improved by meditation." There.

Now, I understand that starting a meditation practice can be intimidating. Maybe you don't know where to start, or how to start. Or you've tried it for a while but couldn't 'stick to it' and got frustrated. I know, I've been there. An easy way to get started is to follow a program, *Balance* or *Headspace* are both very good options.

My best tip is to start very small. Think, 3 minutes. And although you can increase the duration as you get more comfortable, it doesn't have to be the end goal. If all you can fit into your day is 3 to 5 minutes and you know that will help you *stick* to your practice, there is no need to make it longer.

Finding the type of meditation that works for you is also key. There are so many to choose from, it can lead to decision paralysis. Here are three types of meditation I have picked specifically for their benefit on enhancing attention:

1. **Breath Focus Meditation** - This is an excellent 'beginner meditation' and when in doubt, I always come back to this. Sit somewhere comfortable, close your eyes, and focus on your breathing, specifically the sensation of the air getting in and out of your nose. Then count your exhales. You can start by counting them up to 5, then when you get more confident, you can get up to 10. Once you've reached that number, start from 1 again. If you lose count, start from 1 again. If your mind drifts off (and it will), gently bring it back.
2. **Mantra Meditation** - In this type of meditation, we focus on one calming word or phrase, repeating it silently while sitting with our eyes closed. I would suggest keeping it short, simple, and in sync with your breathing. A classic example is to say "let" on the inhale and "go" on the exhale. But you could pick "peace", "calm", "love" or "I am" on the inhale and "enough" on the exhale, or even better, come up with one that is particularly relevant to you at the moment.
3. **Body Scan** - This is a type of mindful meditation. Once you're sitting with your eyes closed, start bringing your attention to your breathing and how your chest and belly rise. Then notice how your body is making contact with the surface beneath you. Then starting from the top of your head, going down to your sole and toes, focus on each part of your body. Pause at each section and notice any sensations like air, temperature, fabric, or pain. Try to simply notice the sensations without labelling them as good or bad. When your mind wanders, bring it back gently without judgement.

Whichever type of meditation you choose, don't try to do it 'right,' simply show up and do it. Apps can be helpful to begin with as they provide guidance which helps sustain attention.

-> Long-term strategy: Starting a Meditation Practice

- Decide which kind of meditation or program you want to start with.

- Assess when and where you're going to practice and put it in your schedule or set up a reminder.
- Commit to practicing for 30 days. If you skip a practice, don't stop, don't beat yourself up, just come back to it.

FINAL THOUGHTS

Now that we've explored the ins and outs of memory, focus, and attention, I hope you're feeling a bit more hopeful about what's possible. No, we can't completely rewire our brains overnight, but we can absolutely strengthen the skills we need to function better day-to-day.

We've looked at a variety of tools—both external and internal—that can help you get there. From prioritizing sleep and nourishing your brain, to experimenting with movement, breathwork, and even brain games, we're building the foundation for long-term change.

So, as we wrap up Week 2, remember that these techniques will take time and practice, and that's okay. You don't need to master everything at once—start small, be kind to yourself, and celebrate the progress, however incremental. The fog won't lift all at once, but bit by bit, you'll find more clarity, focus, and ease in your daily routines. Take a deep breath (or 10). You've got this, and I'm right here with you as we continue this journey together.

Now, what do you always need to do after exercising? Stretching! Well, our brains are no different. So next, in the neuro-gym, we're going to discover how we can stretch our brains to enhance cognitive flexibility.

KEY TAKEAWAYS

- **Sleep is Non-Negotiable:** Getting at least 7 hours of sleep is crucial for improving working memory and focus. Prioritize good sleep habits, and you'll see immediate benefits in your executive function.
- **Fuel the Brain:** What you eat affects how well your brain works. A balanced diet rich in protein, healthy fats, and whole foods helps stabilize your mood and sharpen your

focus. Processed foods and sugar? Not so much. Hydration is equally important.
- **Move Your Body to Boost Your Brain:** Regular aerobic exercise can enhance attention and decision-making. It's not about hitting the gym if that's not your thing—find activities you enjoy, like dancing, hiking, or even hula-hooping, and your brain will thank you.
- **Train Your Brain with Cognitive Tools:** Dual N-Back training, proven to sharpen working memory and improve attention, is a great tool to start with. You can also use strategy games like chess or learn something new, like a language. Apps like *Elevate* offer exercises designed to train memory, problem-solving, and focus. And if you're feeling fancy, neurofeedback therapy is another option. The key to success here is consistency.
- **Breathe and Meditate for Clarity:** Breathwork and meditation are powerful tools to reduce stress and improve focus. Simple practices like box breathing or body scan can calm your nervous system and help you stay on task. Regular practice is best, but even a few minutes before starting a challenging task can make a difference.

week 3: flex your neurons

HOW TO FIND RELIEF WITH COGNITIVE FLEXIBILITY

WITH OUR BRAIN workout under our belt, let's move on to the second principal component of executive function: cognitive flexibility. Or, in our case, the lack of, a.k.a. cognitive rigidity. Cognitive flexibility's key characteristic is adaptability, often described as problem-solving, resilience, and creative thinking

> Wait, what? Creative thinking? But I thought creativity was one of the positive traits of ADHD?!

> Yep! I felt the same way.

When I first heard that, I was furious, as creativity is usually at the top of the ADHD qualities charts. So, I immediately discarded the idea as ludicrous. Hold on… could this be my very own cognitive rigidity in action here, unable to hold two concepts at the time? Probably. Let's dive a little deeper.

While creativity focuses on imagination and originality, cognitive flexibility is about adaptability and problem-solving. And while creativity involves generating multiple ideas, cognitive flexibility requires taking different perspectives. Wait… did I just stretch my cognitive muscles by switching between different concepts here? Possibly.

One thing is sure: when I'm going to start describing what cognitive rigidity looks like in everyday life for adults with ADHD, you're going to start mentally ticking those boxes.

1. ADHD AND COGNITIVE FLEXIBILITY

Cognitive rigidity and ADHD symptoms are a lot more intertwined than they might seem at first, and they have a huge impact on productivity and emotional regulation. Do you struggle with task initiation? That could be your poor cognitive flexibility, making it tricky for you to switch between tasks. Do you burst into tears or get very defensive when someone gives you feedback? That might be your cognitive rigidity, struggling to take another viewpoint and accepting that adjustments are needed. Want to know how cognitively flexible you are? Let's assess.

-> Assessment: Cognitive Flexibility Impact on Your Daily Life

Instructions: *For each statement below, please rate the frequency with which you experience these situations using the following scale:*

0 = Never
1 = Rarely
2 = Sometimes
3 = Often
4 = Always

- *How often do you feel stressed or overwhelmed when your daily routine is unexpectedly changed (e.g., a meeting is rescheduled or your usual commute route is blocked)?*
- *When you are deeply focused on a task, how often do you find it difficult to switch to another task when interrupted (e.g., being asked a question by a colleague or family member)?*
- *How often do last-minute changes to plans (e.g., a dinner plan cancelation) cause you significant anxiety or frustration?*
- *When you receive unexpected criticism or feedback, how often do you find it challenging to accept it and adapt your approach accordingly?*

- *How often do you struggle to change your plans or opinions when presented with new information that contradicts your previous beliefs or plans (e.g., new data or ways of working at work)?*
- *When faced with a new problem, how often do you find it difficult to think of different ways to solve it and instead prefer to stick to one approach even if it isn't working?*
- *How often do you feel overwhelmed or stuck when having to juggle multiple tasks at once (e.g., managing household chores while preparing for a work presentation)?*
- *In social settings, how often do you find it hard to adjust to changes in conversation topics or social dynamics (e.g., shifting topics or adapting to group interactions)?*
- *How often do you find it difficult to move past negative emotions or adjust your emotional responses to fit different situations (e.g., letting go of anger or frustration)?*
- *When you need to make decisions quickly, such as choosing what to do next during a busy day, how often do you feel stuck or unable to consider different options effectively?*

Scoring:

0-10: *Cognitive rigidity rarely impacts your daily functioning.*
11-20: *Occasionally, cognitive rigidity affects your ability to adapt, but it's generally manageable.*
21-30: *Cognitive rigidity regularly affects various aspects of your life, leading to noticeable challenges.*
31-40: *You frequently face significant difficulties due to cognitive rigidity, affecting personal, social, and professional areas.*

See what I mean? Cognitive rigidity can really sneak up on you, right? It's one of those things that quietly interferes with everything —from how you handle feedback to how you deal with last-minute changes. The good news? Once we start recognizing how it's showing up in our lives, we can begin to shift it. The more we work on cognitive flexibility, the easier it'll get to transition between tasks, handle criticism without spiraling, and roll with life's curveballs. So, let's not waste any time.

2. STRETCH IT OUT

No, I'm not talking about stretching ourselves thin here; we're already doing a lot of that. I've got more good news: last week, you've already picked up a lot of tools that not only strengthen your brain but also stretch it. Think of it as the yoga and pilates of the brain, stretch and strengthen all in one. So, you might want to consider them if you haven't added them to your toolkit yet. So, let's take another quick look at them for their cognitive stretching benefits now.

Two for One Brain Training

If you're a fan of feeding two birds with one crumb and making any change you're making count, you could consider one of those five strategies recommended last week:

1. **Exercise** can help cognitive flexibility through neurogenesis, the process of creating new brain cells. It can also improve connectivity between neurons, modulate dopamine levels, reduce cortisol, the stress hormone, and increase endorphins, a mood booster. The list goes on.
2. **An ADHD Diet**, rich in protein, omega-3s, and fiber, ensures a constant supply of energy to the brain, promotes neurogenesis, and maintains a healthy brain environment for neuroplasticity.
3. **Sleep** promotes synaptic pruning, the process of removing less valuable neural connections and strengthening the important ones, which enhances the ability to switch between tasks. Sleep also helps clear neurotoxins and rebalance neurotransmitters, including the ADHD A team: dopamine, noradrenaline, and serotonin.
4. **Breathwork** enhances brain function by elevating oxygen, promoting neuroplasticity, and rebalancing our favorite neurotransmitter: dopamine!
5. **Brain Cross-Training** - Whether you're picking an old school game like chess or puzzles that will help you practice multitasking and encourage strategic thinking, or you decide to download a swanky app, brain cross-training

can strengthen neural connections, and improve neuroplasticity, benefitting both your working memory and your cognitive flexibility. If you want to go down the technological route, check the apps *CogniFit*, *Mind Games*, *Luminosity*, and *Peak*.

EVERYDAY ATHLETE

Just like with working memory, you can practice cognitive flexibility without adding another chore to your to-do list. Cognitive stretching is also a mindset, a way of looking at life and ourselves. With the assessment earlier in this chapter, you've gained a deeper understanding of how your cognitive rigidity might manifest itself. This self-awareness is crucial to initiate change.

One of the first strategies you might want to consider is to lean into your cognitive flexibility and embrace the challenge of flexing next time you have an opportunity. Although the more you practice and the more you become aware, the bigger the transformation will be, frustration might start shading off quite quickly.

-> *Quick win: The Flex Challenge*

1. **Wait for the challenge opportunity** - Let's say Leila canceled our plans for tonight, and I was really looking forward to it.
2. **Define the challenge as precisely as possible** - In my case, "I get very frustrated and emotional when friends cancel plans."
3. **Define the feelings** - In my story, I feel frustrated, disappointed, and rejected.
4. **Analyze this**! Because I can't write a book without throwing some Madonna lyrics in there. Extra points if you can guess which song that's from.

Back to the point, Estelle!!!

Oh, yes, sorry.

What I mean by "analyse this" is why does it feel challenging? So, in my case, it's something like "Now it's too late for making other plans, I've been working alone from home all day so I was looking forward to going out and socializing".

5. **List the possible benefits** - This means I could reframe it as "I could finally give myself that pedicure I've been meaning to. I could catch up on the phone with a friend who lives abroad. I could get an early night. I could batch cook and do other chores that my future self would thank me for, and I would have more time over the weekend for socializing."
6. **Shift your perspective** - That's where the challenge becomes an opportunity. In my example, the loss of social time becomes a gain of me-time. If all else fails, it is always a learning opportunity.
7. **Repeat with the next opportunity.**

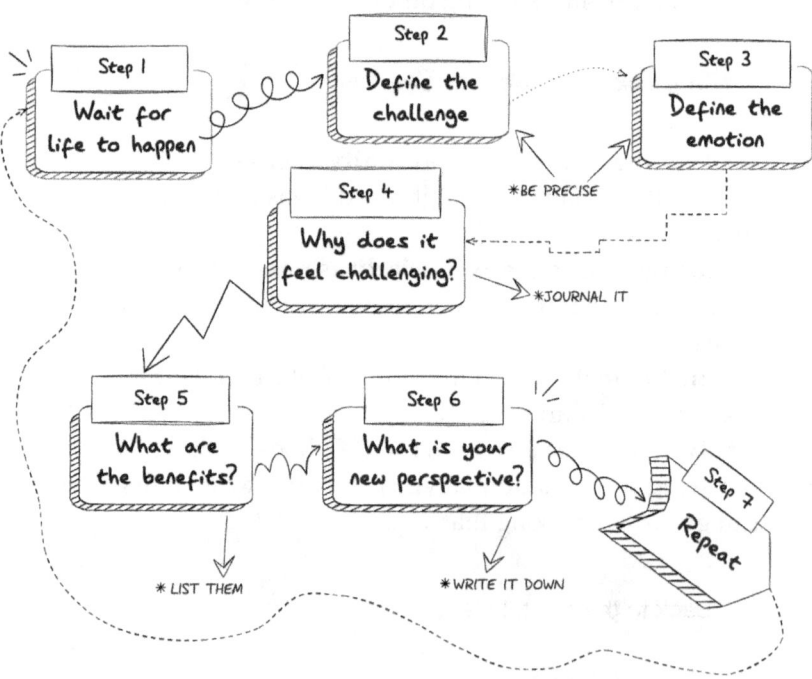

To see this reflective process broken down into seven steps might make it look like a big endeavor, but with practice, it can become second nature and take as little as two seconds to recognize why you're upset, shift your perspective, and move on.

Flex Your Routine

Routine is drilled into ADHDers as the best thing for time management, organization, emotional regulation, and pretty much everything. Rightly so, and I'm guilty too of suggesting routines for every minute of our life.

But here is the downside, setting extremely precise routines will lean into our cognitive rigidity and can send frustration and anxiety to the next level when life just doesn't fit into our plans. Luckily, it is easy enough to correct and something to keep in mind when creating any routine, plan, or schedule.

We are going to scrutinize planning and scheduling a great deal in the coming weeks, but for now, let me share with you one of my favorite hacks: the 'Flexible Day.' I came up with it out of a personal inability to take my Fridays off. I tried to take my Fridays off for months if not years. I could tell my brain needed the time to recharge, but I was getting inevitably drowned in doing more research or "just finishing this urgent task I didn't get a chance to do and wanted to tick off."

So, I decided that Friday could just be a day where I "take it easy." I can work if I want, and I always do a little bit. But it takes a bit longer to get ready. I often go to a yoga class. I usually go out for lunch or a walk with my partner or friends. Overall, it is a day more about nurturing and input than output, pressure, and harsh deadlines. It's more about what I feel like doing and less about what needs to be done. Do you like the sound of that? Enjoy!

> -> Quick win: Set Up a Flexible Day

- **Pick it**: Consider your current commitments and pick a day with fewer obligations and a lighter workload. Weekends can be an option if your work doesn't allow that flexibility,

but it might not be the easiest time if you live with a partner or family.
- **Set an Intention**: This should be very loose, don't be tempted to start a to-do list here. So, for me, it is about nurturing and usually a time for learning, research, and reflection. Your focus could be relaxation, exploration, connection, etc. And you're allowed to switch, of course! That's extra stretching points. If it helps, you can keep a list of possible activities, but no scheduling, okay?
- **Check-in**: In the morning, assess your energy level and mood.
- **Set Boundaries**: If needed, set boundaries, particularly around emails and social media, if you think they are getting in the way of your intentions.
- **Adjust**: Reflect and make any necessary adjustments. Maybe it is not the right day, or perhaps you need a second day. Two flexible days are allowed! My Saturdays are flexible, but I spend them with my family, so they are different types of flexible.

> But that sounds more like a long-term strategy to me, right, Estelle?!

> I agree.

It is one of those quick wins that is also a long-term strategy. If it serves you well, it could become a tool for life. But it is also incredibly quick to set up, and you can get some benefits after one single day. Speaking of long-term strategies, let's take a look.

3. LONG-TERM STRETCHING

Okay, friends, we've tackled some quick wins, but now it's time to get into the long game. Think of these tools as the slow burners of personal growth, like planting seeds that, with time and care, turn into big, strong trees.

Cognitive Behavioral Therapy (CBT)

If you've read *The Empowering ADHD Workbook for Women*, you know everything about cognitive distortions, and you have gone through my system to reframe them. Cognitive restructuring is at the core of CBT, the mother of all evidence-based behavioral therapies. You can often find it as a component of other therapies, such as Dialectical Behavior Therapy (DBT) or Emotional Freedom Technique (EFT).

In fact, we used it earlier with the Flex Challenge when we shifted our perspective from missing out on an evening out to gaining some well-needed personal time. This type of reframing can be used more systematically to tune down the negative self-talk, regulate emotions, and boost self-esteem. Well, guess what? When we do that, we practice cognitive flexibility.

We'll have more CBT exercises in the following week, but if it is something you think you could benefit from doing more systematically, consider investing in behavioral therapy. Before we talk about how, let's check another one.

Dialectical Behavior Therapy (DBT)

While CBT is presented as the holy grail of cognitive therapy for ADHDers and has a special place in our toolkit, DBT has stolen my heart. Why? Because it is invaluable for neurospicy individuals and can help adults with ADHD with about anything, but particularly with emotional regulation.

How? Because cognitive flexibility is embedded at its core. In fact, it's even in its name. DBT stands for Dialectical Behavior Therapy. Let's look up "dialectics" in the Merriam-Webster. It is "the opposition between two interacting forces or elements."

In the case of DBT, the tension is between acceptance and change that both co-exist in the therapy and goes under the name of "walking the middle path." By accepting our ADHD selves while working on changing our unhelpful behaviors, we are stretching our brains further than any ballerina doing split mid-air.

WALKING THE MIDDLE PATH

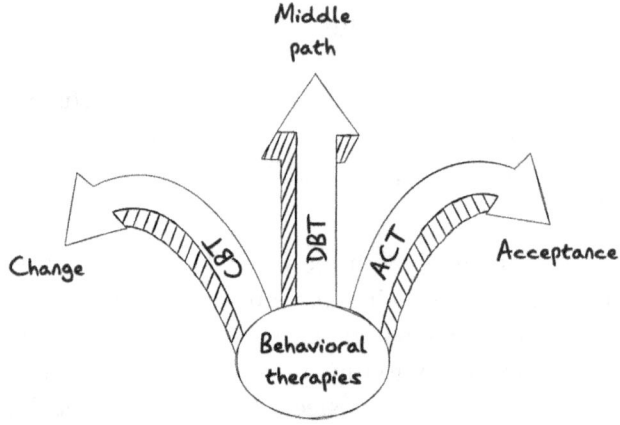

DBT brain stretching offers incredible life skills as we become better at balancing opposite needs, such as self-validation and acknowledging errors, working and resting, things we need to do and things we want to do, emotional regulation, and emotional acceptance. That's why I'll pepper DBT principles and tools throughout this program.

Want to drill down on DBT? Great idea! It can be a heavy investment in terms of time and money. Originally, DBT included weekly 1-to-1 therapy sessions, weekly skills group workshops, and telephone coaching. But since its invention in the 1980s by Marsha Linehan, it's been trialed successfully in more flexible settings. Several researches, including the 2016 Morgenstern study, have shown effectiveness in DBT skills-only settings on adults with ADHD.

-> Long-term strategy: Finding the Right Behavior Therapy setting

- Start by asking your healthcare provider if you could get a referral. Depending on where you live, it could be part of your ADHD treatment.

- Reflect on whether you would like a complete therapy package or just the group skills workshops. Some providers even offer workshops on a particular subject like emotional regulation, relationships, or coping with distress. Similarly, with CBT, would you like individual consultation or group therapy.
- Reflect on whether you would like pure CBT, DBT, or finding a therapist or a coach that integrates some elements.
- Reflect on whether you would like the sessions to be in person or online.
- Research: ask around! That's the trickiest part. Start with people around you: friends and ADHD forums can be a good resource. If you don't know where to start, you can check the DBT-Linehan Board of Certification for DBT. Otherwise, depending on when you're reading this, I might offer CBT and DBT-inspired workshops, so you can check my website.

MINDFULNESS

Another core element of DBT is mindfulness.

> But we've already talked about meditation last week?

> Ah ha, yes! But it's not the same. I know where the confusion might be coming from. Let me explain.

You might have heard of mindful meditation. It is an excellent tool for improving working memory and cognitive flexibility. So, if none of the meditations mentioned in Week 1 take your fancy, mindful meditation might be just the ticket. Actually, mindful meditation and mindfulness as a whole are good for executive function in general: improving attention, promoting emotional regulation, stress reduction, curbing impulsivity, you name it!

Mindfulness goes beyond mindful meditation. It is the act of being fully present in the moment, paying close attention to our experiences, and observing thoughts and emotions without judgment. It strengthens our prefrontal cortex, helping us switch between tasks; it reduces our Default Mode Network activity and reduces mind-wandering, often leading to thought rigidity; it enhances neuroplasticity and reduces stress. No wonder mindfulness has grown in popularity, especially among ADHD folks!

In an article in *Cognitive and Behavioral Practice* in 2015, John Mitchell looked at mindfulness-based interventions designed for ADHD patients and found that "current empirical studies support the rationale for application of mindfulness to ADHD, [...] and provide promising preliminary support for its efficacy."

So, how do we go about it? Besides practicing mindful meditation, you can turn any activity into a mindful one. For a quick win, rebrand any of the following activities as "mindful" by asking yourself questions that can help you tune into the experience, like what does it feel like, what does it sound like, what does it smell like? When your mind starts wandering, let go of the thought without judgment and bring your mind back to the experience.

-> Quick win: Mindful Daily Moments

- **Mindful Eating**: Focus on the taste, texture, and the feeling in your stomach from hunger cues to fullness.
- **Mindful Walking or Running**: Double up with your exercise tool and tune into the sensation in your feet, the vibrations in your body, your surroundings, the smells, etc.
- **Mindful Housework**: Any chore can become mindful, from the running water on your hand when washing up the dishes to the delightful sound of hoovering.
- **Mindful Waiting**: Leave your phone in your pocket and turn a possibly frustrating moment into an opportunity to focus on your breathing, notice the air temperature on your face, the tension in your legs, etc.
- **Mindful Self-Care**: As you shower, brush your teeth, or apply deodorant, instead of letting your mind wander, pay attention to the feelings in your body: the temperature of the water, the smell of the deodorant, etc.

Of course, those will pay off more the longer you practice. Still, they are quick wins as they don't involve carving any time out of your schedule. Mindful cooking might be the key to a less stressed family dinner with regulated emotions. If you're the kind of person who would rather follow a program, you could try one of those long-term strategies.

-> *Long-term strategy: Mindfulness Programs*

- *The Mindfulness Prescription for Adult ADHD* is an eight-step program specifically designed for people with ADHD. It teaches simple, powerful techniques like mindful speaking and listening, body awareness, and sitting meditation.
- *Headspace* is more focused on mindful meditation but is a great starting point. It also has a 'move' section.
- *Balance* is an excellent alternative to Headspace and offers the first year for free at the time of writing. It has tailored programs and a learning mindful meditation program. It also has single tracks, including one for ADHD.
- *InsightTimer* can be overwhelming because of its wide choice. Still, it can be a great platform to find a mindfulness teacher.
- **DIY it**: Speaking of teachers, you could look for a mindfulness teacher near you. Some practitioners have group sessions and can also offer one-to-one sessions if you want something more personalized.

FINAL THOUGHTS

Alright, let's wrap up Week 3, shall we? If you've made it this far, you've stretched your cognitive muscles and, let's be real, probably noticed a few "aha!" moments along the way. Cognitive rigidity shows up in more ways than we realize. But cognitive flexibility isn't some elusive skill reserved for zen masters or superhumans. With the right tools, you can stretch your thinking, adapt better when life is not playing ball, and even reframe those frustrating moments into opportunities for growth.

This week, we took on everything from short-term exercises like the Flex Challenge and mindful daily moments to long-term strategies like CBT, DBT, and mindfulness programs. These aren't just fancy acronyms—when practiced regularly, these powerful tools will help you build resilience, shift your perspective, and, yes, get a little more flexible—both mentally and emotionally.

Now that we've got our brain conditioning covered and are getting mentally fighting fit, let's turn to the other challenges we're facing when it comes to executive function.

KEY TAKEAWAYS

- **Cognitive Flexibility and ADHD**: Cognitive rigidity is closely linked to ADHD symptoms, impacting everything from task initiation to emotional regulation and handling feedback. Recognizing where it shows up can help you make lasting changes.
- **Two-for-One Brain Training**: Last week's tools (exercise, an ADHD-friendly diet, good sleep, breathwork, and brain cross-training) do double duty. They don't just strengthen your working memory and attention; they stretch your cognitive muscles too.
- **Everyday Flexing:** When life doesn't fit into our carefully planned schedules, it's easy to spiral. Try quick-win strategies like the Flex Challenge and a Flexible Day to practice cognitive flexibility in your everyday life and reframe frustrations into opportunities.
- **CBT and DBT** are proven behavioral therapies that help reframe negative thinking, reduce emotional intensity, and build cognitive flexibility. DBT is especially powerful for emotional regulation and helps cultivate cognitive flexibility as we can work on growth while embracing our ADHD quirks.
- **Mindfulness Practices**: Mindfulness isn't just meditation (though that's awesome, too). It's about staying present during everyday tasks, like eating or walking. If you want to dive deeper, there are some great programs —whether you're into apps or books.

week 4: mastering space

5 ADHD-FRIENDLY PRINCIPLES TO CREATE A SPACE THAT WORKS FOR YOU

WHEN IT COMES to organizing space, you would think that all the pixies in the world have gathered around our cradle, cursing us with the plague of leaving a messy trail behind us wherever we go. Why can't we just see the mess around us until it is all we can see, and by then, it is so overwhelming we can't even start?

Well, guess what? Messiness in adults with ADHD is a direct result of our impaired executive function. So we might as well throw in the towel, right? Wrong! That's not why you've picked up this book, and that's not why I've written it. So roll up your sleeves and take the elbow grease out of the cupboard; we're going to discover how to master space the ADHD way…

1. CARVING A MIDDLE PATH THROUGH THE FLOORDROBE

Let's keep flexing our neurons right now and apply *walking the middle path* to our organizational difficulties, by learning to accept our messy tendencies while picking up tools and strategies to work on the crucial areas.

LET GO OF SOCIETAL EXPECTATIONS

Besides our neurological impairments, we live in a world that praises order. Were you shouted out for not tidying up your bedroom as a child? Were you called a slob? Messy? Dirty? Is it currently a source of conflict at work or in your relationships? What was possibly accepted as a child becomes unacceptable as an adult. Have you ever shied away from inviting someone home because you were too embarrassed by what your house or room looked like? Did you ever get a sudden burst of energy and give tidying up your best shot? Blitzed everything, then let it go back to yet another level of disorganization. You're not alone.

And the worst thing about all of that is that you might have internalized these as failures and character flaws, impacting your self-esteem and creating stress, which in turn exacerbates difficulties with organization. Yes, it is that vicious circle again!

So, that's where the acceptance part comes in. Forgive yourself and reframe these so-called 'failures' for what they are: symptoms.

> You mean, I need to accept I will always live like a slob, Estelle?

>> No. I mean, it's not a character flaw but you might never be Mary Kondo.

>> However, you can make your space functional. Want to see how?

> Yes, please!

>> Great! Let's do this!

Ch-Ch-Changes

You also want to consider whether part of your messiness might be a coping strategy. For instance, I grew up leaving important things at the entrance to make sure I would pick them up on my way out. Sure, my school bag could have lived neatly under my desk in my bedroom, but I would have left it there most days.

So, is all mess bad? Why shall we change? And as David Bowie would have said, shall we "turn and face the strange"? Why can't we just be our messy selves?

Let me make one thing very clear: we can! If the physical chaos around you doesn't bother you, overwhelm you, or leave you frazzled, or is not a source of conflict or social isolation, don't change. Not for society's sake.

But if you're struggling to work because your workspace looks like a bombshell, if waking up to a sink full of dirty dishes is grinding you down, or if not finding a clean matching top to your trousers is knocking your confidence down before a job interview, help is on the way. And as always, before we throw ourselves into solutions, we need to assess how much help we need and in which department.

-> Assessment: Disorganization Impact on Daily Life

Instructions: For each statement below, please rate the frequency with which you experience these situations using the following scale:

0 = Never
1 = Rarely
2 = Sometimes
3 = Often
4 = Always

- **Home Environment:** How often do you find it difficult to locate items you need at home due to clutter or disorganization?
- **Work Productivity:** How frequently does disorganization impact your productivity or performance at work?
- **Stress Levels:** How often do you feel stressed or overwhelmed by the disorganization in your personal spaces (e.g., home, car, workspace)?
- **Social Impressions:** How frequently do you worry that others will judge you negatively for being disorganized?
- **Time Management:** How often does disorganization cause you to be late for appointments or miss deadlines?
- **Financial Management:** How frequently has disorganization led to financial repercussions, such as missed bill payments or incurring late fees?
- **Daily Routines:** How often does your disorganization affect your daily routines, such as meal preparation or managing personal hygiene?
- **Mental Health:** How often does the clutter or disorganization contribute to feelings of anxiety or depression?
- **Physical Health:** How frequently does disorganization prevent you from maintaining a healthy lifestyle (e.g., regular exercise, proper nutrition)?
- **Relationships:** How often does disorganization cause conflicts or issues with the people you live with (partner, family, friends, or roommates)?

Scoring:

0-10: Disorganization rarely affects your daily life.
11-20: Disorganization occasionally causes problems, but they are generally manageable.
21-30: Disorganization regularly affects various aspects of your life, leading to noticeable challenges.
31-40: Disorganization strongly influences your daily life, causing significant difficulties in multiple areas.

2. KEY CONCEPTS

Sure, I could take you room to room and tell you what to declutter, but it would be a book about decluttering, not executive function. I'm not sure it would be very ADHD friendly either. Plus, that would be giving you fish, and I'd rather teach you how to fish. So, let's go through some key concepts and how to apply them to our ADHD world.

Minimalism

I know I had a dig at Mary Kondo earlier. Still, she definitely has a point about minimalism: less stuff is easier to tidy. Period. Mic drop. There is no avoiding it, so you might as well accept it now.

Does it mean your decor has to look like it's coming out of a Muji catalog? No, and we'll cover style later. It means that if your approach to worldly possessions is guided by the core philosophy of minimalism, it will make your organization easier.

Minimalism focuses on what is essential in your life and discarding the rest. It emphasizes quality over quantity by reducing items that serve a similar purpose or are not versatile. And there is also intentionality or the famous "does it spark joy" or is it just taking space and, even worse... is it stealing attention?

In practical terms, it might mean that your working space is streamlined to a clean desk with a computer, a notepad, and a pen, and everything else that is not for daily use gets out of sight. How relaxing does it sound?

Or, if you want another example, take my favorite hack to banish your floordrobe for good (you know, that pile of clothes on your bedroom floor), which I explain in great detail with step-by-step instructions in *Empowering Books for Women with ADHD*, is to adopt a capsule wardrobe with a maximum of 50 items. Not only does it create space and simplify laundry, but it drastically reduces decision fatigue: less choice means fewer decisions.

So, besides the mathematical proof that fewer items are easier to clean and organize, for people with ADHD, less clutter can also reduce overwhelm and increase calm.

> Okay, Estelle, I'm game, I feel a sudden urge to declutter right now!

> Great! Even though minimalism is a long-term strategy for managing physical chaos, let's surf this wave of enthusiasm with some decluttering challenges for a quick win!

-> Quick Win: Decluttering Games

- **30-Day Minimalism challenge**: I'm starting with the hardcore one! Declutter one item on day 1, two items on day 2, three items on day 3, etc. And yes, 30 items by day 30! At the end of the month, you will be 465 items lighter.
- **27 Fling Boogie**: Find 27 items to get rid of in 15 minutes.
- **Feng-Shui Time Attack**: It's the shorter version of Fling Boogie. Find 9 items to declutter within a maximum of 5 minutes. Playing with friends or family? Whoever finishes first is the winner.

FUNCTIONALITY

Another organization's key concept is functionality. We've already touched upon it when exploring minimalism by prioritizing items that can serve multiple functions. But as a concept, functionality goes further and is highly relevant for creating an ADHD-friendly space. Let me introduce you to zoning.

Zoning is practiced by giving each space a purpose. Depending on your priorities and needs, you could create a work zone designed for focus and productivity, a relaxation zone where you can unwind, and a sleeping zone where you can... well, sleep! You might even want to add an exercise zone or a hobby zone.

And no, you don't need to live in a mansion to practice zoning. In a small apartment or room, the work zone can be a desk, the relaxation zone can be an armchair, and the sleeping zone can be your bed. Then, your fitness zone could be a chest at the bottom of your bed that contains a yoga mat, dumbbells, and headphones. And your hobby zone could coexist with your work zone, with equipment stored under your desk.

Zoning has multiple benefits for us folks with ADHD. First, it helps us find a space for things and hopefully will help us find them later. It also helps with task initiation through conditioning. For instance, "bed is for sleeping" is often given as a top priority advice when struggling with insomnia. Here are some zones you might want to consider:

- Work/Study Zone
- Relaxation Zone
- Sleeping Zone
- Dining Zone
- Cooking Zone
- Fitness Zone
- Hobby/Craft Zone
- Laundry Zone
- Utility Zone
- Reading Nook
- Meditation/Wellness Zone
- Entertainment Zone
- Social Zone
- Children's Play Zone
- Outdoor Zones (Gardening Zone, Outdoor Dining Zone, Play Area, etc.)

You definitely don't need all those. So consider which ones you need and where to establish them. Then, use this knowledge as your compass for organization.

-> Long-term Strategy: Defining Zones

1. **Make a list of all your activities**: Daily, weekly, and occasional ones, such as working, sleeping, eating, relaxing, exercising, and hobbies.
2. **Prioritize:** Determine which activities require dedicated space due to their frequency or importance. Identify any activities that cause particular stress or distraction problems.
3. **Analyse Space**: Walk through your home and note the characteristics of each area. Consider factors like natural light, traffic flow, size, and proximity to other zones.
4. **Map out:**
   a. **Primary Zones:** Designate specific areas for high-priority activities like working or sleeping.
   b. **Secondary Zones:** Identify areas for activities that are important but less frequent, such as hobbies or exercising.
   c. **Flexible Zones:** Consider spaces that can be adapted for multiple uses, like a reading nook and meditation zone or an entertainment and social zone.

Before you start moving all the furniture around the house, finish reading this chapter so we can address the *why*. Why should we be zoning?

Clarifying zones can help with task initiation and general overload when organizing. Functionality teaches us to give a space to everything so we know where to find them, particularly items that tend to go missing, like keys and wallets. When giving something a place, think, "Where would I go looking for it spontaneously? Where do I use it most? Which zone does it belong to?"

Now, sometimes there can be a bit of tension here, but that's okay; it's an opportunity to practice cognitive flexibility. For instance, you might think that deodorant belongs in the bathroom, a.k.a. 'your self-care zone.' But if you tend to put it on just before getting dressed, maybe it belongs in your 'dressing up zone.'

To make a space functional, you also want to streamline your system. Give easy access to things you use often. If we keep the deodorant as an example, maybe not only does it belong in your 'dressing up zone,' but its place could be with your underwear. You're the only one who can decide. What can sound like a crazy organization to someone might be the answer to smashing B.O. issues for someone else.

When designing space, we also have to consider ergonomics. It is often overlooked in ADHD treatment but could be a great addition to a holistic approach to managing your symptoms. You might want to invest in an adjustable standing desk, a sit-stand stool, or a bean bag chair.

> Now, it's all well and good, but I still want my home to look good.

> Fair enough! I'm getting to it.

Enter our last key concept: Aesthetic.

AESTHETIC

Actually, in an organizational context, aesthetics doesn't simply refer to making your interior "look good." It is about how an environment makes us feel and can influence our emotions and behavior. So, given our sensitivity to sensory inputs, it turns out to be a pretty important concept that can reduce stress, enhance our mood, and promote focus.

Natural light is critical for boosting mood, and if you remember Week 2, we might be struggling with our circadian rhythm. A 2017 study published in the *Journal of Psychiatric Research* found a "successful use of Bright Light Therapy for advancing melatonin phase and improving ADHD symptoms in adults." I have set up a solar light bulb on my desk for a couple of years now and have found an improvement in my mood, particularly during dark English winters.

But on the other hand, "many adult outpatients with attention-deficit/hyperactivity disorder (ADHD) report an oversensitivity to light," 69% of us actually, as reported in *Frontiers in Neurology*. More research is needed on the relationship between light and ADHD, but you can decide to be more intentional with your lighting. Tune into your responses and test what suits you best. The solution might be to layer the types of lighting and adjust them according to the time of day, mood, and emotions.

A neutral palette can reduce visual stimulation and promote concentration. Blues and Greens are said to promote calm and relaxation and are often used in bedrooms. On the other hand, bright colors energize and might be good to use as an accent in your fitness zone or parsimoniously in your work zone.

Consider your sensitivity to sound. If the noise of people running up and down the stairs triggers you while trying to relax, besides noise-canceling headphones, you might want to consider carpeting the staircase.

3. GET ON WITH IT

Ever wished you were Mary Poppins and could just click your fingers, and all the toys in the nursery would jump into the toybox? Well, thanks to this technique, I'm about to show you, that is exactly what is going to happen. Just kidding. It's not going to happen. Sadly, I have no fairy dust to give you to magically tidy it all up, and that's where we need to work on the acceptance part.

Now for the change part, the fairy dust could be someone you pay to do it for you, and if you have the means and feel comfortable with that, go for it. Whatever works for you. But for most of us, the 'magic' change often lies in getting started. But just before you run off with a sudden urge to do the dishes, let's add a little bit of intention. That's the secret sauce to sticking with it in the long term.

-> *Reflections: The Biggest Impact*

- *What area causes me the most stress or anxiety? Consider which part of your home frequently frustrates you or contributes to feeling overwhelmed.*
- *Where do I spend most of my time?*
- *Which zone is easiest to declutter?*

- *What clutter is affecting my focus the most? Reflect on which physical items or arrangements distract you the most during daily activities.*
- *Where can I make changes that will improve my routines? (e.g., preparing meals in the kitchen, getting ready in the morning, or completing work tasks.)*
- *Which area of my home do I avoid because it's messy?*
- *What space would I benefit from the most from being decluttered? For instance, clearing a workout area might encourage more regular exercise, and tidying up the living room might mean you invite friends and feel less lonely.*
- *How does the clutter in each area affect my emotional well-being?*

Thanks to these reflections, you should have a pretty good idea of where to start. If you're now really itching to reorganize your whole bedroom because you've realized the mess there is impacting your mood, and this is your relaxation and sleep zone and you know exactly how you're going to rearrange it and what you're going to get rid off, go for it! Put the book down, and come back once the novelty has worn out.

And if you're feeling overwhelmed and have zero energy to start, keep reading. You're in the right place, as we're going to look at how to get started.

-> Quick-win: The Smallest Surface

1. With your previous reflections in mind, pick the zone that would most immediately impact your life positively.
2. In this zone, think about the smallest area that would have the most significant impact and why? Only pick one! For instance, in the cooking zone, is it the sink because it wears me down when I don't even have a clean mug to pour myself some coffee in the morning? Or is it the countertops because as soon as I see that clutter on them, I am instantly discouraged from cooking a healthy meal? Then I'm winding myself up while cooking, and I end up angry with everyone at the dinner table.
3. Commit to clearing this surface and keeping it clear for a

whole week. It should be so small that it shouldn't take you more than 5 minutes daily to keep tidy.
4. Schedule when you're going to do it. For instance, "After dinner, it will be clear when I wake up the next day, and I can feel smug while grabbing a clean cup of coffee."
5. After a week, reflect and add either the next logical step in the same zone. Repeat in another zone if you feel this zone is not overwhelming anymore (no need for perfection).

By having a sense of priority and letting go of societal expectations for perfection. Organizing space becomes a gradual and regular process.

4. LOST PROPERTY

ADHD is a losing game, and, yes, it sounds like an Amy Winehouse song, and it can be just as painful, especially if sentimental value is attached to something you've lost. If you've read *The Empowering ADHD Workbook for Women*, you know all about my engagement ring.

We are infamously prone to losing our belongings, and besides the emotional distress comes the frustration and embarrassment that come with it. Just thinking about it, I can feel the mom's guilt of sending my kids to school without their school bags, just because my brain was setting the world right that morning. But hold on a second?... That book bag is not lost... It's forgotten! Another category under the "managing belongings" label. And then there is stuff that is 'lost temporarily' or, as we'll call them, *misplaced*. They can be gone for days, weeks, sometimes years, but they reappear.

And guess what's to blame for this unhelpful behavior? Yep, the very reason we're here: our executive dysfunction. Let's name and shame:

- **Inattention** is when we're not in the moment while placing an item.
- **Poor Working Memory** means we can't remember where something was last placed, which compounds the issue.
- **Our impulsivity** can shift our focus to the next task before collecting items we were just using. Poor organization

means items don't even have a place to return to. But we've got that covered now: minimalism means few items to lose, and zoning can reduce misplacing and forgetting belongings.

Does it mean you're never going to lose things again? Sadly no. And that's where the acceptance mindset comes in.

When (not if) you lose something, before you go on blaming negative self-talk or burst into tears, evaluate how bad the consequences are. If it is something you can easily replace or won't impact your life, acknowledge the feelings (anger, frustration, shame?), then brush them off with an "oh well," and think about whether there is a particular situation that led you to lose it. If so, think about how you could avoid repeating the situation next time. If it does have sinister consequences or feels really painful, acknowledge the feeling and work on forgiving yourself. Then again, think about what led to it and whether there are any tools you could use next time to avoid it.

Talking of tools, long-term strategies we've covered in earlier chapters, such as CBT, DBT, mindfulness, and meditation, will contribute to a lower frequency of lost and misplaced items by enhancing attention and working memory while reducing stress levels. Practicing mindful transitions is an excellent way of using mindfulness to minimize the trail we leave behind. And as you know, transitions can be a tricky one for us.

-> Quick Win: Mindful Transitions

1. As you leave a place, **pause**: stop what you're doing, whether you're looking at your phone or having a conversation.
2. Take a moment to **breathe**.
3. **Observe** and check while being fully present that you're not leaving anything behind.
4. Check that you have whatever essentials with you (key, wallet, phone, ID)

Making this a habit and anchoring it to any departure will minimize the amount of stuff you lose.

FINAL THOUGHTS

If you're feeling a little less overwhelmed by the idea of taming the chaos around you, then we're in good shape! We've explored why messiness is a part of our ADHD world, how it's not a character flaw, and most importantly, how we can work *with* it.

We're not aiming to become minimalist gurus or organization ninjas overnight. Instead, it's about creating functional spaces that support our brains, not stress them out. We've learned to let go of societal expectations (no more shame in that floordrobe!) and embrace the tools and strategies that will help us take control of our environment, one small surface at a time.

From zoning our spaces to practicing mindful transitions, we're setting ourselves up for success on our own terms. It's not about perfection, it's about progress. So, whether you're starting with decluttering one drawer or finally finding a place for that pile of papers on the kitchen table, know that every small step adds up to big changes over time.

Now, roll up those sleeves, pick one area, and let's get to work. Next week, we'll look at time, a very powerful ally of space!

KEY TAKEAWAYS

- **Messiness and ADHD**: Our mess isn't a personal flaw—it's executive dysfunction doing its thing. So, let's stop beating ourselves up over it. Accepting our messy tendencies while working on realistic strategies can also help us practice cognitive flexibility. We're not aiming for perfection—just functionality that doesn't leave us feeling overwhelmed.
- **Minimalism Saves the Day**: Less stuff = less mess. It's not about living in a sterile, dull space. It's about making life easier and reducing the mental overload of constantly managing too many things. Plus, fewer choices = less decision fatigue.

- **Zones, Zones, Zones**: Create zones in your space! Assign different areas for specific activities, like a work zone, a chill-out zone, or a chaos-free sleep zone. It's like setting mental boundaries that help you function better.
- **Functionality Over Fancy**: Organize based on what makes sense for *you*. Forget Pinterest-perfect. If your deodorant belongs in your closet, go with it! Tailoring your space to your habits will make staying organized easier.
- **Vibe Check**: Aesthetic isn't just about pretty spaces—it's about creating environments that feel good and support your ADHD brain. Think of natural light, calming colors, and tuning into what makes you feel at ease.
- **The Art of Losing Things**: Let's be real—losing things is part of the ADHD package. Instead of spiraling into self-blame, recognize it as a brain blip. We can't avoid it entirely, but we can reduce how often it happens with a little mindfulness and organization.
- **Mindful Transitions**: Avoid the lost keys drama by practicing mindful transitions. Take a beat before you leave a space, check your essentials, and make it a habit. It's a simple trick, but it can save you from a lot of frantic searching later.
- **Start Small, Build Momentum**: Don't let the clutter monster overwhelm you. Pick the smallest surface that will have the biggest impact and focus on keeping it clear for a week. Baby steps, my friend. We're playing the long game here. If you need a boost to get started, play a decluttering game.

week 5: mastering time beyond the clock
HOW TO FIND BLISS IN TIME MANAGEMENT

TIME MANAGEMENT and ADHD often evoke images of missed appointments and chronic lateness. Yet, I never felt they were a serious issue for me. I even used to take offense a bit when it was hinted that we, ADHD folks, are bad with time. I am never late! Okay, admittedly, I like to arrive fashionably late to parties, but that's intentional. However, I was rarely the one to be late for work and rarely missed a deadline. In fact, the pressure of a looming deadline was usually what spurred me into action. Like the time I spent the entire night before my English Literature exam reading *The Ambassadors*, a feat that, although successful, triggered an ophthalmic migraine. Was this good time management? Well, no.

For those of us navigating life with ADHD, managing our hours isn't just about clocking in on time. It's about untangling the complex web of how we perceive and engage with time itself. You would have guessed it, it is all to do with our executive function, from working memory to impulsivity.

1. THE TRUE FACE OF TIME MANAGEMENT WITH ADHD

So let's take a look at ADHD and time, beyond the social courtesy of being punctual. It involves grappling with a unique set of challenges that is down to a misunderstanding of our own capabilities and needs. A 2019 study in *Medical Science Monitor* on perception of time in ADHD concluded that "individuals with ADHD have difficulties in time estimation and discrimination activities as well as having the feeling that time is passing by without them being able to complete tasks accurately and well."

The Intricacies of Time Blindness

Let me introduce you to *time blindness*—a phrase that struck a chord with me. It is about the sheer inability to accurately sense the passage of time—a problem that isn't exclusive to ADHD. It can affect people with brain injuries, for instance, but it is often a signature trait of ADHD.

For many of us with ADHD, time blindness isn't just a minor inconvenience; it's a huge roadblock when it comes to managing our time. We often think we've got way more time than we do. For example, I'll tell myself something will take an hour, and before I know it, four hours have vanished. And it's not just about work—it messes with everything from our daily routines to how we handle responsibilities, ultimately taking a toll on our productivity and well-being.

Time with ADHD feels elastic. When there's plenty of it, we're moving through molasses. But as the deadline approaches, everything accelerates. This erratic pacing is not just about working against the clock; it's about how the perception of time changes based on deadline proximity, impacting everything from workflow to stress levels. And remember what stress does to us?

Hyperfocus

Hyperfocus is another wild card in the deck of time blindness. Once we're deep into a task, pulling ourselves out is just as hard as getting started was. It's that all-consuming tunnel vision that can make us forget the basics—like drinking water. That's why you hear me say, "Keep a water bottle on your desk" or "Use an app to remind you to hydrate."

Hyperfocus doesn't just make us forget to take breaks; it can also derail us from other important tasks. Something less exciting but with an earlier deadline often gets pushed aside. This constant juggling between what interests us and what we're obligated to do is a classic ADHD struggle, made even trickier by our warped sense of time.

As always, the road to better time management starts with understanding where we're at and what we need. For Sophie, it might mean escaping the endless cycle of procrastination. For Elijah, it could be about preventing burnout. Wherever you're starting from, recognizing that is the first step to making lasting changes.

-> Assessment: Time Blindness Impact on Daily Life

Instructions: *For each statement below, please rate the frequency with which you experience these situations using the following scale:*

0 = Never
1 = Rarely
2 = Sometimes
3 = Often
4 = Always

- **Meeting Deadlines**: *How often do you miss deadlines for assignments or projects at work or college?*
- **Punctuality**: *How frequently are you late for meetings, appointments, or social engagements?*
- **Time Estimation**: *How often do you underestimate the time needed to complete tasks, leading to rushed work or missed obligations?*
- **Long-term Planning**: *How frequently do you struggle with planning for future events or deadlines, such as saving for a vacation or preparing for an examination?*
- **Daily Scheduling**: *How often do you find yourself running out of time to complete your daily activities?*
- **Personal Care**: *How frequently does poor time management affect your ability to maintain personal care routines, such as eating, sleeping, or exercising regularly?*

- **Social Relationships**: *How often does your timekeeping cause misunderstandings or frustrations with friends and family?*
- **Professional Impact**: *How frequently do you feel that your difficulties with time management limit your career or educational opportunities?*
- **Leisure Activities**: *How often do you miss out on or are unprepared for leisure activities due to losing track of time?*
- **Stress and Anxiety**: *How often does your inability to manage time effectively lead to increased stress or anxiety?*

Scoring:

0-10: Time blindness rarely affects your daily life.
11-20: There are occasional issues caused by time blindness, but they are generally manageable.
21-30: Time blindness regularly affects various aspects of your life, leading to noticeable challenges.
31-40: Time blindness strongly influences your daily functioning, causing significant difficulties across multiple areas.

Once you've recognized and accepted where your time management difficulties might be, we can start to look at tools and strategies that can help.

2. TIME MANAGEMENT FROM THE OUTSIDE IN

The world around us is not short of productivity gadgets to bip and blink at us to try to keep us on track, and some of them have their place in an ADHD toolkit. Let's take a look.

-> Quick-win: Calendars and Reminders

A digital calendar with reminders is the baseline, and my guess is that if you're interested in executive function, this is something you've got covered. If not, download one right now. There are plenty of free options, most of which come with your phone or email, which can help you get fancy with it and use integrations. And do yourself a favor, have the same calendar for everything, work and personal, or have a place where all your calendars are synchronized; otherwise, it is a sure road double-booking yourself and forgetting appointments.

Personally, setting my digital calendar to alert me half an hour before events has been a lifesaver. This buffer isn't just about catching my breath; it's about mentally preparing for the shift from one task to the next—essential for someone who doesn't transition smoothly.

> -> *Quick-win: Watching Time Tick By*

If you're someone who spends a lot of time at their computer and can get lost in the minute details of writing a report and agonize for hours in the indecision of whether you should use Garamond or Helvetica, a screen countdown timer might help. And, yes, of course, the answer is Helvetica. As a sans-serif, it is more neurodivergent-friendly.

> Okay, fonts are awesome, Estelle, but that's really not the point.

> Oh, yes, thanks. ADHD diversion! Back to time management.

A countdown clock on your computer is a gentle yet firm reminder that time isn't infinite. It can anchor us into reality but also break down time into manageable chunks of productivity. This visual reminder can help us stay on track without being overwhelmed, turning a potential stressor into a motivator. You'll find plenty of free online options and might have one already integrated into your computer.

If you're more an 'on your feet' kind of person but can as easily lose track of time, investing in a big digital watch with a countdown timer function could be money well spent.

> -> *Quick-win: Time management apps*

If you've read any of my previous books, you know how much I love *TickTick*. It is way more than a to-do list and the free version is pretty generous, while the full singing and dancing one is very affordable. You can prioritize your tasks and schedule them for when you need to be reminded. There is no point in jotting down on an endless to-do list, "Buy new school shoes for the kids," when I'm thinking about it on the beach on July 25. I know I won't have an opportunity to get the kids to the shop and get their feet measured before August 28, so that's when I set the 'to-do' for. I want it out of my head but also out of my *today's* to-do list. With *TickTick*, I can jot it down, even dictate it, on the beach and ask to be reminded on August 28. You can also schedule regular reminders for habit-building and tracking.

Now, if you're like me and your issue with time blindness is about estimating how long things take and you want to hop off that conveyor belt feeling of constantly chasing the end of your daily tasks, the app *Motion* might be the answer. The downside is that it isn't cheap and is very much a computer-based app tailored to people who are at their desks most of the time. But it has transformed my relationship with time simply by combining a to-do list with a calendar, and then it acts like a PA and organizes your schedule, lovely!

But you have to give each task a time estimation. Ouch! During the first week of using it, I actually real-life cried, realizing I had to double my time estimation if I wanted to get anywhere close to a manageable day. Of course, you could do that manually in your diary, but the beauty of Motion is that it will schedule it automatically for you depending on the deadline and importance. And if you don't get around to it because you know, life happens… then it will reschedule it automatically for you.

3. TIME MANAGEMENT FROM THE INSIDE OUT

While these tools are invaluable, they are just part of the equation. The true art of managing time with ADHD involves a more profound synthesis of external aids and internal understanding. It's about seeing these tools as extensions of our intentions, helping us shape our days with purpose and presence. This integration is not a one-size-fits-all but a personalized strategy that evolves as we do and a perpetual journey of adjustment and learning. So, let's turn to more transformative strategies.

ADHD Friendly Routine

I feel a bit like a broken record when it comes to routine because I've been banging on about it so much on so many different platforms that I feel I have said everything there is to say on the subject. Still, I come back to it because this is such a transformative cornerstone of managing life with ADHD.

While essential tools like calendars and reminders lay the groundwork, a well-structured routine can profoundly impact our ability to manage time effectively. This isn't about rigidly segmenting every hour but about understanding the flow of our lives and creating a flexible framework that accommodates both our needs and responsibilities.

-> Long-term strategy: Crafting a Calming Routine

Are you sold yet? Let's craft your unique routine.

1. **Time audit**

Creating a routine starts with clearly assessing your personal and professional landscape. This means considering various factors such as living arrangements, caregiving responsibilities, and work commitments. Are you a parent managing school runs? Are you self-employed and juggling multiple projects and clients? Each of these scenarios will significantly shape your routine. Dump everything on a page.

2. **Weekly routine**

Grab a weekly calendar. Start by sketching a weekly schedule by adding what can't be moved. It might be your work hours or children drop off and pick up time. And let's not forget about sleep. Yes, sleep must be scheduled: pick a regular bedtime and wake-up time, then add both winding down at night and getting ready in the morning.

Once these unchanging commitments are mapped out, it's time to consider the critical but shiftable tasks. These might include house cleaning, personal hygiene, meal preparation, eating, and grocery shopping. Now, my young self would have found it so lame to have a house cleaning time in my weekly plan, but it's saved my family from endless arguments, blame games, and living in chaos. On Sunday morning, we all clean and tidy up. We each know what we've got to do and get on with it with no whining or tantrums, neither from the kids nor the grown-ups.

If you're unsure how long these tasks actually take—because, let's face it, time estimation can be a challenge—double your estimated time. This might seem excessive, but trust me on this one, it provides a realistic buffer and reduces the stress of underestimating. To refine your estimates, consider tracking your activities. Apps like *Toggl Track* offer a straightforward way to measure how long tasks truly take without relying on guesswork.

3. Incorporating Joy

But hey, it's not all about the musts and shoulds. Ensure your schedule includes time for rest, hobbies, and activities that bring you joy. These aren't just frivolous additions; they're essential for mental health and overall well-being. Also, think about incorporating habits that contribute to your personal growth and transformation—these should also find a spot in your weekly plan while helping you check whether you might be overstretching yourself.

As ADHD creatures, we tend to crave novelty, too, so leaving space to try new activities can go a long way in making the routine sustainable.

4. Building in Buffers and Flexibility

Remember cognitive flexibility? While it's crucial to have a structured plan, flexibility is key. I've already told you about my Fridays, so remember to pick a flexible day. Life isn't predictable, especially with ADHD. While I know we do housework on Sunday mornings, and hair washing is on Sunday night, I have no routine on Saturday or Sunday afternoon. And, of course, we might be invited to a party on a Sunday, and things get reshuffled for once.

While mapping your tasks, incorporate buffers throughout your day—short periods set aside for transitioning between tasks or unexpected events—can prevent the whole system from derailing when interruptions occur.

Remember, a routine for someone with ADHD is more than a set of tasks and timelines—it's a living framework that respects the finite nature of time and our unique ways of processing it. It's about crafting a schedule that doesn't just fill time but enriches our lives, accommodating both our ambitions and the quirks of our neurodivergent minds while managing stress. This approach isn't about cramming tasks into an already bursting schedule; it's about accepting reality and living life on life's terms while making time work for us.

In the context of executive function, the finitude of time also translates into how much attention and energy we have on a given day or week. The Spoon Theory can be very helpful when planning to accept our limitations and explain them to others.

4. TIME AS ENERGY: THE SPOON THEORY

Have you come across people on social media labeling themselves as *spoonies* or saying how they have "used all their spoons?" It comes from *The Spoon Theory*, a metaphor created by Christine Miserandino to explain the experience of living with chronic illness. Miserandino, who has lupus, developed the theory to illustrate the limited energy reserves available to those with chronic conditions, comparing them to a finite number of spoons. Let's break it down.

So, spoons are a metaphor for energy, and we all start our day with a limited number. Then, as we go about our day, activities cost spoons. Work, of course, but think also about cooking, washing your hair, socializing, and commuting. When you live with a limited amount of spoons, you learn to decide which task you must prioritize that day to manage your spoons. You can also learn techniques to replenish your spoons, like taking a nap or practicing deep relaxation.

So, while the term *spoonies* was initially invented for people with chronic illnesses and physical disabilities, it's grown in popularity among communities of people who experience limited energy.

Now, a myth about ADHD is that we have boundless energy. It may physically appear so, but mental fatigue is real, and the fact that we might be chasing dopamine at 2 am doesn't mean that our cognitive spoons were not totally depleted by 3 pm.

In our ADHD world, spoons can be a helpful metaphor to describe our limited amount of mental energy. The cognitive effort we have to put into tasks that demand concentration and organization uses more spoons and often leads to decision fatigue. Similarly, emotional regulation can use up a lot of spoons and leave us unable to complete seemingly simple tasks.

Assessing where you need the most spoons and how you can manage them throughout the day can be an extremely helpful guide when establishing a routine and planning your day.

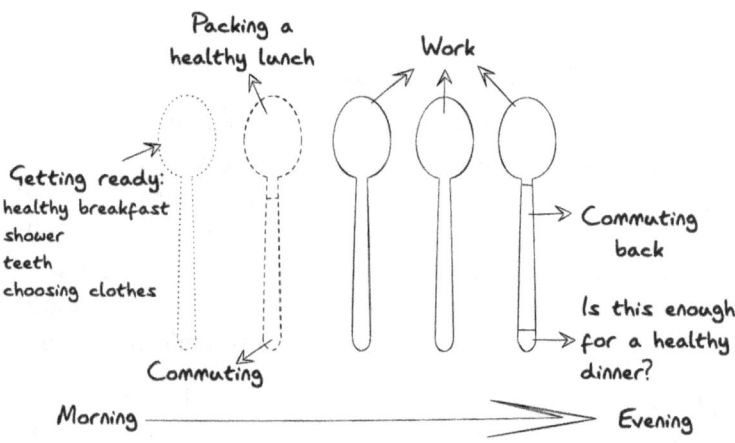

-> *Reflections: Spoon usage*

- *What tasks require the most energy for me? Which activities drain my energy the fastest and require the most effort to complete?*
- *What time of day do I feel most energized and focused? When am I most alert and capable of tackling demanding tasks during the day?*

- *How do my energy levels change after certain activities or interactions? How different types of engagements (social, professional, leisure) affect my energy. Which ones leave me feeling drained, and which ones might replenish my spoons?*
- *What daily habits or routines contribute to losing my spoons more quickly? Identify patterns or specific behaviors that tend to deplete your energy faster than others.*
- *How can I better distribute my spoons throughout the day to avoid running out? Consider scheduling high-energy tasks during your peak times and allowing for breaks or less demanding activities when your energy is lower.*
- *What strategies can I implement to conserve or regain spoons during the day? Think about restorative practices or environmental changes that might help you maintain or increase your energy levels.*
- *How do unplanned events or interruptions impact my spoon allocation? How do they affect my energy, and how could I handle these disruptions better to conserve my spoons?*
- *What signs show that I'm running low on spoons, and how can I respond proactively? Think of fatigue or being overwhelmed, and consider what proactive steps you could take to manage your energy before it depletes completely.*
- *How do stress and emotions affect my spoon levels? What emotional management tools might help me preserve my spoons?*
- *What changes can I make to my environment to help me better manage my spoons? Consider adjustments in your physical or social environments, such as organizing your workspace, limiting noise, or setting boundaries with others regarding your availability.*

Understanding time in terms of tasks vs energy is a massive step toward sustainably improving productivity.

FINAL THOUGHTS

Alright, folks, here's where we tie a bow on this week's deep dive into time management with ADHD. It's easy to get caught up in the image of missed deadlines and being late for everything, but that's not the whole story. Sure, many of us might struggle with time in the traditional sense—arriving on time, estimating task durations, or keeping up with schedules—but there's more to this puzzle.

Time management for us is about understanding *how* we relate to time. It's not just a matter of staring at the clock; it's about learning how to manage our energy, avoid burnout, and set up systems that actually work for our unique brains.

From embracing time blindness and tackling hyperfocus to building routines that flex with life's unpredictability, we've covered it all. The tools are out there—timers, apps, and calendars—but it's also about tuning in to your inner rhythm. Managing time isn't just about ticking boxes; it's about making life feel more manageable, less stressful, and ultimately more fulfilling.

And now that we've explored how to organize our space and manage our time, we're primed to dive into the next big challenge: productivity. With the groundwork we've laid, we can now build strategies that take all this newfound clarity and put it into action. So, get ready! Next up, we're tackling how to be productive in ways that work for us, not against us.

KEY TAKEAWAYS

- **Time with ADHD Isn't Just About Being Late:** Time management for us is also about navigating the weird ways we perceive time—from everyday routines to long-term goals—and how that impacts our productivity, stress levels, and energy.
- **Time Blindness**: With ADHD, sensing the passage of time can feel impossible. We often think we have more time than we do, and suddenly, hours disappear. It's not just annoying—it can seriously derail our day. Time either stretches out like molasses or speeds up when the pressure's on. Learning to navigate this erratic pacing can help reduce stress.
- **Hyperfocus Can Be a Double-Edged Sword**: While it's great to get into the zone, hyperfocus can lead to ignoring other deadlines, responsibilities, or even basic needs like eating or taking a bathroom break. Managing it is crucial to find balance.

- **Using External Tools**: Whether it's a trusty digital calendar, a timer, or a time-management app like *TickTick* or *Motion*, external tools can help us stay on top of things when our internal clock needs help, but it's only one piece of the puzzle. Also, using a countdown timer on your computer or watch can be a lifesaver. It's a gentle nudge to remind us that time is still ticking—even when we're lost in the details.
- **Routines That Work for Us**: A well-crafted routine isn't just about squeezing more into the day—it's about building a structure that fits our ADHD brains. Flexibility and buffer time are crucial for preventing burnout and overwhelm.
- **Energy as Spoons**: Time isn't just about hours—it's about energy. Understanding the Spoon Theory helps us pace ourselves, ensuring we don't burn through our cognitive and emotional energy too quickly.

week 6: healthy productivity

HOW TO ACHIEVE GOALS WITHOUT BURNOUTS

When we hear "productivity tips," we often conjure images of highly organized individuals effortlessly managing their tasks and time. But what if the conventional wisdom on productivity not only falls short for those of us with ADHD but actually nudges us toward burnout?

When I first ventured into a creative career about twenty years ago, I became utterly fascinated by productivity. I devoured every book and tried every method under the sun, packing my weeks with to-do lists and crushing the Pomodoro like I was making salsa for an army. Initially, it felt empowering—I was getting so much done! No more procrastination stations. But one crucial function was missing from my productivity playbook: the pause button. Without it, my efficiency wasn't just unsustainable; it was unhealthy.

> But I'm fatigued
>
> I can't add another technique
>
> My life is too full

> I know, I've been there, and I see you
>
> That's why we have to find another way. Let me show you

The truth is, productivity strategies don't often translate well for the ADHD brain. We might dive into hyperfocus and churn out work at an impressive rate, but at what cost? The ability to work like a machine doesn't mean we should, especially when long-term sustainability is at stake. While tools are helpful, understanding how to use them in a way that respects our unique brain wiring is crucial.

In this chapter, we'll explore productivity strategies that genuinely work for us and discuss how to tailor these tools to fit not just our tasks but our lives and mental health. Healthy productivity isn't about pushing harder; it's about working smarter and creating routines that honor our needs, rhythms, and, yes, our ADHD. By the end of this chapter, my goal is for you to have a toolkit that suits your specific challenges and the wisdom to know when and how to hit pause, recharge, and sustain your productivity without sacrificing your well-being.

1. THE FACE OF PRODUCTIVITY WITH ADHD

Let's backtrack for a minute. What does productivity really mean, especially for us mere mortals with ADHD?

At its heart, productivity is about effectiveness—how effectively can we use our time to achieve what matters most to us? It's not just about doing things quickly or ticking as many boxes as possible; it's about doing the right things in the right way.

> Yeah, okay, great, Estelle. But how exactly?

> Excellent question, my neurospicy friend!

> Let's find out.

Productivity can be split into several components:

- **Prioritization**: Yep, that's a tricky one and the cornerstone of productivity. It's about figuring out which tasks deserve your immediate attention and which can be delegated or deferred. It's deciding what's crucial for reaching your goals and what's just noise.

- **Time Management**: Once we've sorted out our priorities, the next piece of the puzzle is managing our time effectively. We've gone over this last week. This involves allocating specific blocks of time to tasks, understanding our own work rhythms (hello, mid-afternoon slumps), and respecting our cognitive load limits (or spoons).
- **Efficiency**: Here's where we look at how we can do things in a streamlined manner. Efficiency isn't about cutting corners; it's about finding smarter, more sustainable ways to get tasks done without burning out our mental engines.
- **Execution**: The best-laid plans are only as good as their execution… This is about taking action and sticking to the plan. For us in the ADHD squad, this might involve employing various strategies to initiate tasks and keep on track. We've mentioned external tools before digital clocks, apps like *Motion* and *TickTick*, or reminders, and shortly we'll look at more internal ones.
- **Adjustment**: Because our lives are not static, our approach to productivity shouldn't be either. It's about tweaking and fine-tuning our methods as we learn more about what works for us and what doesn't, as well as adjusting to new life circumstances.

It's essential to recognize that even within the ADHD community, we are not all the same. Our struggles with productivity vary widely depending on numerous personal factors. For example, while I once battled with procrastination, these days, it's a rarity for me—except perhaps when it comes to life admin tasks and bureaucracy. Work-related tasks and routine life chores generally get done.

However, I continuously wrestle with managing my energy levels and dealing with fatigue. This is mainly due to my caregiving responsibilities; my cognitive functions are still in high demand even after my workday ends. For someone else, with a less routined life and fewer responsibilities, the challenges may be flipped—it could be that procrastination remains a significant hurdle while energy management is less of a concern. So, how about we take a look at your personal struggles so you know where to focus your effort when it comes to productivity?

-> Assessment: Productivity Gaps

Instructions: For each statement below, please rate the frequency with which you experience these situations using the following scale:

0 = Never
1 = Rarely
2 = Sometimes
3 = Often
4 = Always

- **Task Completion:** How often do you have difficulty completing tasks you've started, especially if they are lengthy or complex?
- **Time Management:** How frequently do you underestimate the time needed for tasks, resulting in missed deadlines, rushed work, or burning yourself out?
- **Distractions:** How often are you distracted by external stimuli or unrelated thoughts when trying to work? (Oh, look another squirrel)
- **Prioritization:** How frequently do you struggle with prioritizing tasks, leading to working on less important tasks instead of urgent ones?
- **Motivation:** How often do you find it hard to start or continue working on tasks that are not immediately rewarding or stimulating, or once the initial excitement wears off?
- **Organizational Skills:** How often do you experience difficulties in organizing tasks, workspace, or digital files, which impacts your work efficiency?
- **Fatigue and Energy Levels:** How frequently do you feel too tired or lack the energy needed to complete a task?
- **Attention Span:** How often do you find your attention waning after only a short period, necessitating frequent breaks or changes in activity?
- **Handling Feedback:** How often does receiving criticism or feedback disrupt your workflow or affect your motivation negatively?
- **Meeting Expectations:** How frequently do you feel that you are unable to meet the expectations of your role due to difficulties associated with ADHD? (Note the emphasis on feel.)

Scoring:

0-10: Your ADHD has little to no impact on your productivity.
11-20: Some ADHD-related challenges affect your productivity but are generally manageable.
21-30: Your productivity is regularly affected by your ADHD, leading to noticeable difficulties.
31-40: ADHD significantly impairs your productivity across various areas, requiring immediate intervention and support.

2. FOCUS ZONES

"I have kept a hotel room in every town I've ever lived in. I rent a hotel room for a few months, leave my home at six, and try to be at work by six-thirty. To write, I lie across the bed, so that this elbow is absolutely encrusted at the end, just so rough with callouses. I never allow the hotel people to change the bed, because I never sleep there. I stay until twelve-thirty or one-thirty in the afternoon, and then I go home and try to breathe; I look at the work around five; I have an orderly dinner—proper, quiet, lovely dinner; and then I go back to work the next morning."

What Maya Angelou describes here in her 1990 interview on The Art of Fiction for *The Paris Review*, is an excellent illustration of what is also known as Focus Zones. It is a strategy used to improve concentration and productivity. It involves designating periods and places where you can work with minimal distractions. And would you like to know the best part? You've already done most of the homework to design your very own Focus Zones.

But why bother? Well, the benefits of boosting productivity and lowering stress are great. Dedicating specific times and places to work can help us complete tasks more efficiently. Clear schedules and dedicated spaces also help minimize the tendency to procrastinate. And by reducing distractions it is easier to maintain concentration on the task at hand. The clear boundaries between work and personal time can also help prevent work from encroaching on personal life, setting healthy boundaries and reducing stress and fatigue.

To return to Angelou's example, she knew she couldn't work at home, so she used a hotel room. She also knew how she liked to write: lying down. She knew that after writing for an extended period, she needed a total break, so she used to wait several hours before fitting in a second focus zone, when she was working on editing, and then would have a proper evening off. That's the level of self-awareness we want to get to when designing our focus zones.

For Angelou, with informed guesses from the rest of that interview, her focus zones would have looked something like this:

1. **Morning Focus Zone** (6:30 AM - 12:30 PM)

   - **Location**: Hotel room
   - **Task**: Writing
   - **Preparation**: Yellow pad, pen, do not disturb sign on the door.
   - **Break**: Quick break with a sherry

2. **Afternoon Focus Zone** (5:00 PM - 7:00 PM)

   - **Location**: Home
   - **Task**: Editing
   - **Preparation**: Writing from the morning, yellow pad, pen
   - **Break**: none

I wouldn't dare compare myself to Maya Angelou. Still, I, too, have 2 focus zones: 2 hours in the morning in my home office where I do my writing and editing, which requires an uncluttered brain and the least distraction possible. Come the afternoon, I need to see people. So, I go to a co-working space with a laptop and noise-cancelling headphones. Being in a space where other people are working helps me get on with my work, and I designate another 2 hours to the less creative side of my business. This technique is called body-doubling. Chatting with other humans (who are not my mentees) during breaks is also essential for my mental health.

But maybe you're more like Anya. She is a consultant who runs workshops, and she's also writing a book to share her techniques. When we first started talking, she was struggling to fit both into her life, particularly to get the writing part done. She also wanted to spend some quality time with her partner. She felt stressed by the pressure of having a big publishing house behind her. The writing needed to happen pronto!

After reflecting and trying different possibilities, she realized she could focus on her writing better late at night when all was quiet. As her partner is a musician and often gigs in the evening, it meant she could spend quality time with him in the morning, knowing she could schedule workshops in the afternoon and do her writing in the evening. So now, her focus zones look like this:

1. **Afternoon Focus Zone** (2 PM - 5 PM)

   - **Location**: Mostly Online (Home office)
     - **Task**: Consulting workshops
     - **Preparation**: Laptop, headphones, notepad, pens.
     - **Break**: 10-minute tea break around 3:30 PM

2. **Evening Focus Zone** (9 PM - 11.30 PM)

   - **Location**: Kitchen table
   - **Task**: researching, writing, or editing
   - **Preparation**: Laptop, notebook, pen, phone off in another room.
   - **Break**: tea break when required

Ready to devise your own focus zones? Let's go!

-> Long-term strategy: Designing Your Focus Zones

1. **Dig Out Your Homework**

Look back at the work you've done in the previous weeks. By now, you should have a pretty good idea of what needs to happen and when it could happen (thanks to your schedule), and thanks to zoning, you will have some idea of where it could happen.

Although the examples and the following steps strongly focus on "getting work done," it doesn't have to be about professional work and study. If you're a waiter and don't need a focus zone at work, maybe there is something else in your life that could benefit from one. It could be exercising, playing an instrument, or learning a language. In fact, taking yourself to the gym to work out is a focus zone!

2. **Productivity Audit**

   - **What times of the day am I most focused and productive?** Reflect on when you feel most alert and engaged. Is it morning, afternoon, or evening? Consider your spoons.
   - **What type of distractions most commonly disrupt my focus?** Identify whether they are auditory, visual, digital, related to physical activity, or just people being around.
   - **Which tasks require my highest level of concentration?** Determine the tasks that need undivided attention and could benefit most from being completed within a focus zone.

3. **Evaluating Your Environment**

   - **What characteristics does my ideal work environment have?** Consider aspects like lighting, noise levels, temperature, and the type of seating that helps you feel most comfortable and focused.
   - **How does the current setup of my workspace hinder my productivity?** Identify any elements of your current environment that make focusing difficult.
   - **Where can I establish a dedicated focus zone in my home or workplace, or do I need to go somewhere else?** Think cafes, the library, etc. If you have a workplace you need to go to, are there any adjustments that could help?

4. **Scheduling the Focus Zone**

   - **Identify when to schedule your focus zone(s):** Grab your weekly routine, the one we created in week 4. Consider both your focus needs and your commitments.
   - **Scheduled Breaks**: Or not. If you have a short focus zone and want to harness hyperfocus without interruption, give

it a go. For some, integrating short breaks to rest and recharge helps maintain focus over longer periods.

5. **Designing the Focus Zone**

   - **What essential tools and resources do I need within my focus zone?** List all the materials you need to accomplish tasks without having to leave the zone. These might include a computer, specific software, books, notepads, noise-canceling headphones, a water bottle, a coffee drip, etc.
   - **What rules do I need to establish for my focus zone to function effectively?** Consider rules about interruptions, like turning the phone off or a firm "no talking to mom while she's writing" rule.
   - **How can I physically delineate my focus zone from other areas?** If your Focus Zone is not a room in itself, consider using room dividers, curtains, or furniture arrangements to create a clear boundary.

6. **Maintaining Focus**

   - **What strategies can I use to minimize distractions within my focus zone?** Explore options like noise-cancelling headphones, website blockers, or a do-not-disturb sign. You can also look at focus strategies like the Pomodoro technique, where you remove all distractions for 25 minutes, then take a 5-minute break, and repeat four times until you take a 20-minute break.
   - **How will I handle interruptions that might occur while I'm in my focus zone?** Plan strategies to manage interruptions, such as having a notepad to quickly jot down interruptive thoughts.

7. **Review and Adjust**

   - **How will I assess the effectiveness of my focus zone?** Think about criteria you can use to measure how well the zone works, such as the number of tasks completed, the level of focus achieved, and how you feel afterward.

- **What adjustments might be necessary if my focus zone isn't meeting my needs?** Be prepared to tweak your setup, schedule, or rules based on what is or isn't working and when life and work circumstances change.

Now that we've covered how to create Focus Zones, it's time to dive into two key players in our ADHD world: hyperfocus and daydreaming. These mental states can be both a blessing and a challenge, depending on how we harness them. So, let's explore how to tap into hyperfocus for productivity and how to manage it when it starts to derail us. And daydreaming? Turns out it's not just for zoning out!

3. HARNESSING HYPERFOCUS AND THE ART OF INTENTIONAL DAYDREAMING

It is rather ironic that those of us branded with the label' Attention Deficit' can, in fact, exhibit an extraordinary level of concentration known as hyperfocus. It's often part of the "you don't look ADHD" package, given that our hallmark trait supposedly revolves around a scattergun attention span. Yet here we are, capable of such deep immersion in tasks that the world might well cease to exist around us.

Attention Displacement

Instead of calling it 'Attention Deficit,' which feels like a total misnomer, I prefer 'Attention Displacement.' We don't lack attention—it's just that we don't always direct it where we're meant to. When we're captivated by something that truly grabs us, we can tune out everything else around us.

The truth is when we're locked in, it's usually because we're chasing that elusive dopamine hit. Our ADHD brains are wired to crave stimulation, and when we find it, it's like striking gold. That rush keeps us glued to the task at hand, and pulling away feels nearly impossible. Add in our struggle with transitions, and voilà—you've got hyperfocus.

From a psychological standpoint, hyperfocus might also be our brain's way of overcompensating for those moments when focus feels impossible. It's like our brains swing wildly from scattered to laser-focused, trying to balance things out. This all-or-nothing way of operating isn't just about finding something fascinating—it's our brain's attempt to hold on tightly when focus has been slipping through our fingers.

This ability to zone in is so profoundly tied to our executive dysfunction, especially our challenge of shifting gears between tasks. That's where establishing Focus Zones comes in handy. By carving out specific spaces and times for deep work, we can tap into hyperfocus more intentionally—even for tasks that aren't exactly thrilling. That's how, with a little structure and practice, we can harness that power.

The Double-Edged Sword of Hyperfocus

However, there's a dark side to this beautiful quality. The intense concentration can lead to neglecting other essential responsibilities —those mundane but necessary tasks like, in my case, paying bills or managing life admin. It can also lead to social isolation, as the desire to continue a rewarding task may cause us to skip social interactions.

And yes, the dreaded burnout is never far off, looming like a storm cloud on a seemingly clear day. That's where the focus zone swoops in to save the day once again by putting a time limit, allowing us not only to harness the power of hyperfocus but also to mitigate some of its drawbacks.

Hyperfocus is a superpower, but as Uncle Ben says, "With great powers comes great responsibility." Understanding hyperfocus and learning how to use it is crucial for anyone with ADHD. It's not just about unleashing this power; it's about controlling it, directing it, and knowing when to dial it back so we don't end up running on empty. Fear not, there is a strategic tool to recharge and reset our brains, preparing us for another deep dive into productivity.

The Power of Daydreaming

Yes, you read that right. Daydreaming is also a power that can be harnessed.

Growing up and even into my early adulthood, I wore the label of daydreamer like a badge of honor—it was part of my quirky charm. However, the charm seemed to wear off as I aged.

I recall a moment in my early 20s when I was in the Underground with my boyfriend. We were sitting, facing each other, having a conversation. Or rather, he was talking, and I was in a world of my own. He suddenly stopped and expressed his frustration over my tendency to drift away mid-conversation. That was the first time I realized people around me could notice and found it hurtful. What was once endearing in a child was now a source of annoyance in an adult. Friends began to echo similar sentiments, suggesting my daydreaming implied I didn't care about them or what they had to say.

Determined to remedy this, I learned to clamp down on my daydreaming in social settings, unknowingly honing my skills in what's known as 'active listening.' Though I maintain that giving someone your full attention is a basic courtesy, I internalized the notion that daydreaming was inherently bad. Only later did I realize how beneficial it could be, especially for someone with ADHD. But just like hyperfocus, it needs to be controlled and directed.

How to put Intention into Daydreaming

I was inspired by concepts like "scatter focus" from Chris Bailey's book *Hyperfocus*, but I prefer to call it *Intentional Daydreaming*. It suggests a more purposeful engagement with our daydreams, devoid of the negative connotations associated with being scatter-brained. By setting aside dedicated times for intentional daydreaming, we can harness this natural inclination for reflection and ideation.

Do you remember from Chapter 1 that daydreaming activates our brain's Default Mode Network, which is most active at rest? So yes, we need to deactivate it to focus. Still, when we don't need to focus, this isn't idle time—it's when our brain busily processes past interactions, makes plans, and engages in creative problem-solving. It's a time when we can process emotions and find restorative mental rest, refreshing ourselves for future tasks. So pretty essential, don't you think?

> Okay, but that's basically mindfulness, right?

> Fair question! Not quite.

In mindfulness, we would let the thought go and refocus on the present moment, e.g., breathing, walking, and eating. In intentional daydreaming, we let the thoughts emerge organically, but we follow and record them. Do you want to give it a go?

-> *Quick-win: Intentional Daydreaming*

1. Set Aside Dedicated Time

- **Choose a Duration**: Start with 10-15 minutes specifically earmarked for intentional daydreaming.
- **Schedule It**: Incorporate this time into your daily or weekly schedule. Consistency is key to turning intentional daydreaming into a productive habit.

2. Create an Ideal Environment

- **Select an Activity**: Choose a low-engagement activity that supports daydreaming. Walking, especially in a familiar environment, works exceptionally well. Alternatively, activities like mindful coloring, cooking, gardening, knitting, or even people-watching in a cafe can also provide the right balance of engagement and freedom for your mind to wander. It works better if it is something you enjoy doing.

- **Set an Intention**: You can free-wheel it and just see what thoughts come up. That's particularly good for processing. Or you can choose a theme. That is great for ideation and problem-solving.
- **Minimize Distractions**: Ensure the chosen activity doesn't involve multitasking or digital distractions. Ideally, you want to turn that phone off.

3. Capture Your Daydreams

- **Keep Tools Handy**: Carry simple tools like Post-it notes and a pen or a small notebook.
- **Record Thoughts as They Come**: Jot down any thoughts, ideas, reminders, or inspirations that arise during your daydreaming session. The act of writing helps in retaining these ideas and also provides a physical log we can review later.

4. Review and Utilize Your Insights

- **Sorting and Categorization**: After each session, take a minute to go through your notes. Sort these thoughts into categories such as immediate tasks, long-term projects, personal reminders, or creative inspirations.
- **Integrate Into Your Life**: Decide which ideas are actionable and incorporate relevant tasks into your to-do lists or project plans. For those ideas that are more about creativity or long-term possibilities, consider how you might want to keep track of them, or not.

5. Reflect and Adjust

- **Evaluate the Process**: Regularly assess how your intentional daydreaming sessions impact your productivity and well-being. Are they helping you solve problems? Are they giving you the mental break you need?
- **Make Adjustments**: Based on your reflections, adjust the frequency, duration, or methods of your daydreaming sessions.

By structuring your daydreaming in this intentional manner, you can transform what many might dismiss as mere distractions into a powerful tool for problem-solving and brain replenishing. This method not only respects the natural workings of the ADHD brain but leverages its unique strengths to enhance personal and professional life.

4. PRIORITIZE LIKE A PRO

If there's one battlefield where those of us with ADHD often find ourselves lost, it's the minefield of prioritization. The ability to sort, sift, and assign importance to our endless tasks list can sometimes feel like herding cats. However, discovering a method that clicks for you can transform you into a lion or cat tamer.

I'm going to share a few well-known techniques that can help, as well as some general rules that apply to all techniques and can help you create your own. Because, just like everything else, it is about finding the one that will work for you. Mixing and matching is also perfectly acceptable.

Step 1: Capturing the Chaos

Whether it's the thoughts from intentional daydreaming or the sudden bursts of "must-dos" that hit us in the shower or when falling asleep, capturing these tasks is crucial. Whether you write them down on Post-it notes, a notebook, or an app like TickTick, the key here is to have a system. And I'm not just talking about work here; it goes for your personal life, too. Just get them out of your head and into the world. I would strongly suggest having one system only that you use for everything rather than one for work, one for personal tasks, or worse, one per project. Don't roll your eyes, I was that person.

Step 2: Sorting Through the Noise

Once you've captured your tasks, you'll need to organize them in some way—and that's the tricky part for us. I know it can feel like trying to solve a Rubik's cube in the dark. But that's where a system that helps us decide what is worth our precious time, attention, and energy can help. So here are a couple for you to try.

-> Quick-win: ABCDE Technique

Let's start with the simple A, B, C, D, E technique that can help bunch those tasks neatly together:

- **A for Absolutely essential**: These tasks are crucial and need immediate attention.
- **B for Basic needs**: Important, but not urgent.
- **C for Could do**: Nice to tackle if time permits.
- **D for Delegate**: Important, but perhaps someone else can do it.
- **E for Eliminate**: These tasks are distractions in disguise. Cut them loose.

Now, depending on your circumstances, that might well be enough. I like its simplicity.

However, it's lacking one important thing: It doesn't consider urgency—a critical factor for those of us dancing on deadlines. Enter the Eisenhower Matrix. And yes, it is named after the 34th President of the United States, who was known to be very productive and apparently used an importance and urgency framework. However, Stephen Covey labeled it the "Eisenhower Matrix" in his book, *The 7 Habits of Highly Effective People*. Okay, so how does it work?

-> Quick-win: The Eisenhower Matrix

The matrix divides tasks into four quadrants based on two criteria: urgency and importance.

Quadrant I: Urgent and Important (Do First)

This is for tasks that are both urgent and important. These are critical for your immediate work or personal life. They can be deadlines for projects, emergency situations, bill payments, exams, and important family obligations.

Action: Do these tasks as soon as possible.

Quadrant II: Important but Not Urgent (Schedule)

This is for tasks that are important but do not require immediate action. These tasks are crucial for long-term goals and success. They could be planning, networking, exercising, self-improvement, research, or check-ups.

Action: Schedule a time to do these tasks.

THE EISENHOWER MATRIX

```
                    Importance
         (Low)
           |  ┌─ Do first ─┐    ┌─ Schedule ─┐
           |  │            │    │            │
           |  │            │    │            │
           |  └────────────┘    └────────────┘
           |  ┌─ Delegate ─┐    ┌─ Delete ───┐
           |  │            │    │            │
           |  │            │    │            │
           |  └────────────┘    └────────────┘
         (High)────────── Urgency ──────────(Low)
```

Quadrant III: Urgent but Not Important (Delegate)

This is for tasks requiring immediate attention but not necessarily important for your personal or work-related goals. It's things like answering basic inquiries, household chores, and logistical arrangements.

Action: Delegate these tasks to someone else whenever possible.

Quadrant IV: Neither Urgent nor Important (Eliminate)

This one is for tasks that are neither urgent nor important. These are the least productive uses of your time. It can be time-wasting activities, some social media activities, busy work, or long email chains.

Action: Eliminate these from your schedule as much as possible.

To implement it, grab your captured tasks and place each task into one of the four quadrants based on urgency and importance. Then, focus on completing Quadrant I tasks first and then schedule Quadrant II tasks. Look to delegate Quadrant III tasks and eliminate Quadrant IV tasks.

By distinguishing between urgency and importance, you can allocate your time and energy more strategically. Using an app like TickTick, which has an Eisenhower Matrix embedded, can streamline this process by allowing you to first capture the tasks in your inbox as they pop into your head, then assign urgency and importance either on the go or when reviewing your day, then find them sorted in the Eisenhower Matrix when it's time to act. Speaking of acting...

Step 3: Get it Done

Now that you have prioritized and know what you should be doing, do it. Thanks to your Focus Zones, you should also have a designated time and place to do it.

Step 4: Review Regularly

Reassess your categorizations regularly, as the urgency and importance of tasks can change over time. That's where daily and weekly reviews step in to help you reflect, prioritize, and schedule what's coming next. And this is where an app like *Motion* can help by doing some of that prioritizing and scheduling automatically.

HOW TO PRIORITIZE

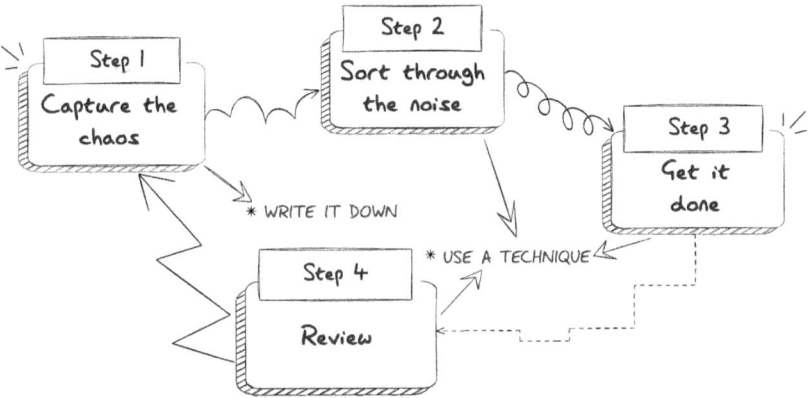

Remember, the best prioritization method is the one that works for *you*. It's about finding harmony in your unique symphony of tasks. If you really want to nerd down on prioritizing, I suggest you also take a look at RICE, which considers Reach, Impact, Confidence, and Effort. This method is particularly useful when dealing with projects where your actions could have disproportionate effects, helping you to focus on tasks that yield the highest rewards for the least effort. Whether in terms of financial return, personal growth, or emotional well-being, prioritizing by potential impact can significantly boost your productivity ROI (Return On Investment, for those unfamiliar with business-speak).

By transforming prioritization from a daunting chore into a personalized strategy, you'll unlock a more focused and fulfilling way to navigate your day-to-day life with ADHD.

FINAL THOUGHTS

We've come a long way this week, haven't we? From rethinking the traditional productivity playbook to building strategies that actually work for our ADHD brains. Healthy productivity isn't about cramming more into your day, squeezing every last drop of energy, or feeling guilty when you don't check every box. It's about creating a life where getting things done doesn't come at the cost of your mental health or well-being.

The truth is, we can't always grind our way to success—especially not when hyperfocus and fatigue tend to be the poles we swing between. But now, you've got some game-changing tools to help you navigate the middle path. You've learned how to prioritize, manage your time, replenish your attention spoons with Intentional Daydreaming, and design Focus Zones that honor your own rhythms. We're leaving behind the days of endless to-do lists that lead to exhaustion and overwhelm and stepping into routines and strategies that allow you to be both productive and kind to yourself.

The ultimate goal? To get what matters done—without losing yourself in the process. So, whether you're battling procrastination, struggling with motivation, or just trying to stay afloat in the whirlwind of daily life, remember that productivity is as much about resting as it is about doing. It's about knowing when to pause, refuel, and come back stronger.

And now that we've mastered productivity, we're ready for the final—and perhaps the most important—chapter of this journey: regulating emotions and impulses. Because, let's face it, ADHD is often an emotional rollercoaster, and managing those big feelings and impulsive urges can be even trickier than time management. So, let's dive in and explore how we can find a little more peace amidst the chaos. You've made it this far—let's bring it home.

KEY TAKEAWAYS

- **Healthy productivity with ADHD** isn't about grinding harder; it's about working smarter using strategies that honor our energy levels and protect our mental health. Traditional productivity hacks can backfire on ADHD brains, often pushing us toward burnout.
- **Focus zones** are dedicated times and spaces where we can really lock in and get things done without distractions. Whether it's a quiet corner of your home, a coworking space, or a cozy café, these zones help us tap into our most productive selves. Knowing when and where you work

best (hello, self-awareness!) can help you build healthier boundaries between work and personal time, reducing stress and boosting productivity.
- **Hyperfocus** is like a superpower with a side of kryptonite. It lets us dive deep, but it can also cause us to lose track of time and neglect other important things. Setting up Focus Zones helps harness hyperfocus in a balanced way so we don't burn out.
- **Daydreaming** is not a waste of time. When used with intention, it can actually fuel creativity and problem-solving as well as replenish our mental spoons. Try carving out moments for intentional daydreaming to let your mind wander in productive ways.
- **Prioritization** is the cornerstone of productivity, especially for ADHD brains, where tasks can feel overwhelming and all equally urgent. Learning to differentiate between what's truly important and what can wait (or be delegated) is crucial. Techniques like the Eisenhower Matrix (sorting tasks by urgency and importance) or the A, B, C, D, E method (labeling tasks from absolutely essential to eliminate) can help organize and simplify your task list. Knowing when to tackle high-priority tasks, based on your focus and energy levels, can help you accomplish more without burning out. Tools like *TickTick* and *Motion* can help.

week 7: emotion regulation and impulsivity

HOW TO PROCEED MINDFULLY

IF YOU'VE EVER WONDERED why your emotions can feel as unpredictable as the weather in spring (in England) or why a slight provocation can send your reactions into a tailspin, you're not alone. For us ADHD folks, emotional dysregulation is directly linked to several key areas of executive functioning and affects 30 to 70% of adults with ADHD, according to the journal *European Psychiatry*.

First, our working memory is not doing its job of being a mental sticky note that reminds us of past experiences to guide our present emotions. For instance, remembering that we managed just fine the last time our friend canceled on us before going out could soothe our current anxieties.

Then we can mention our cognitive flexibility again, you know, our mind's agility in shifting perspectives and adapting emotions. Well, flexibility would allow us to look at situations through different lenses. Understanding that our friend is worried sick about her gerbil and needs to take the poor rodent to the emergency vet could potentially ease the intensity of our emotional response to the cancellation.

Luckily, we've strengthened both of those in previous weeks. What we need to cover now is the direct link between our emotional tempests and our inhibitory control, or rather, the lack thereof. Impulsivity is the unwelcome spark that ignites swift, intense reactions before rationale can catch up. Understanding and managing our impulsivity is crucial because it lays the groundwork for strengthening our emotional regulation. It's about learning to pause, reflect, and choose responses that align more closely with who we aim to be—rather than reactions that flare up and fizzle out, leaving confusion and chaos in their wake.

The good news? This is Week 7, and by now, you're equipped with an arsenal of tools from our journey together. There is a reason this chapter comes at the end. The skills and strategies we've developed over the previous chapters—decision-making, problem-solving, planning, and prioritizing—are not just isolated tools. They are integral to taming impulsivity and enhancing emotional regulation. Each skill enhances our ability to pause between stimulus and response, giving us the space to choose how we react.

1. UNDERSTANDING IMPULSIVITY IN ADHD

Impulsivity is a bit like a mischievous inner gremlin that just loves to press the "do it now" button, often before we've had a chance to consider what we're doing. And here's the kicker: it doesn't just show up when we burst into tears or snap at someone in a Monday morning meeting. No, impulsivity is sneakier than that. It can pop up in everyday life, often in ways that can feel socially awkward—or, let's face it—socially unacceptable.

But before we dive too deep into 'fixing it,' let's take a moment to reflect. Now, just like in previous weeks, we're not looking to shame ourselves into change. The real goal here is to understand why we want to curb our impulsivity in the first place.

Maybe there is more than society telling us we *shouldn't* interrupt or that we *shouldn't* blurt out our thoughts mid-meeting. Because, hey, we're rebels, who cares about society, right? Okay, we care. A lot. But maybe the other reason is that horrible feeling that washes over us after we've said something sharp, only to realize later that we either got it wrong or overreacted, and in many cases, both. Wanting to change because you don't want to feel awful anymore? That's real. And it's a much better motivator than feeling like we have to play by society's rules. Because, in effect, we don't.

Poor inhibitory control goes beyond blurting out in conversations. Sometimes, it's making decisions on a whim—whether that's quitting a job with no plan, buying something wildly out of budget, or even leaping into a new relationship before the dust of the last one has settled.

There's also the risky behavior side of impulsivity, which is no joke. This can range from substance use and reckless driving to compulsive eating. For some of us, it's reaching for the nearest snack before our brains have even caught up to the decision. So, yeah, impulsivity has a way of showing up in all kinds of places, and none of them tend to end well.

Let's circle back to *why* we want to work on this. Is it because you're tired of feeling embarrassed? Or because you regret a spur-of-the-moment decision the next day? Let's assess which areas of our lives are most affected by impulsivity. Whether it's conversations, spending, or relationships, identifying the patterns is key. Only then can we figure out why we want to change and what strategies will help us stick to that change.

-> Assessment: Impulsivity's Impact on Your Life

Instructions: For each statement below, please rate the frequency with which you experience these situations using the following scale:

0 = Never
1 = Rarely
2 = Sometimes
3 = Often
4 = Always

- **Decision Making:** How often do you make decisions impulsively without considering the consequences?
- **Work Tasks:** How frequently do you start new tasks at work before finishing ongoing ones?
- **Adhering to Rules:** How often do you find it difficult to follow rules or guidelines because of impulsive actions?

- **Attention to Detail:** How frequently do you rush through tasks, leading to mistakes or incomplete work due to a lack of patience?
- **Handling Criticism:** How frequently do you respond impulsively to criticism or feedback?
- **Social Interactions:** How often do you find yourself interrupting others during conversations or reacting without thinking in social settings?
- **Emotional Responses:** How often do you react impulsively to emotional situations that you later regret?
- **Eating Habits and substance abuse:** How often do you find yourself eating impulsively, choosing unhealthy food options without thinking, or reaching out to alcohol or other substances when you promised yourself you were not going to?
- **Spending Habits:** How frequently do you engage in impulsive buying or spending money without planning?
- **Driving Behavior:** How often do you engage in impulsive driving behaviors, such as speeding or making sudden lane changes?

Scoring:

0-10: Impulsivity and inhibitory control rarely affect your daily life.
11-20: There are occasional challenges related to impulsivity, but they are generally manageable.
21-30: Impulsivity regularly affects various aspects of your life, leading to noticeable difficulties.
31-40: Impulsivity and difficulties with inhibitory control strongly influence your daily functioning, causing significant challenges.

2. JUST STOP

Are you cringing at the *just*?

> Well, yeah, Estelle, if only I could, I wouldn't be buying your books, would I?

> I know. I know. Let me elaborate before interrupting!

I know the *stop* is the tricky part. Still, it is also the cornerstone of shifting from screaming, "That's a hill I'm ready to die on," while in tears, to having a constructive conversation about what's bothering you and finding an acceptable solution. It's not easy, but it's worth it, and luckily, besides the long-term strategies we've explored already, some techniques can help.

S.T.O.P.

Unsurprisingly, STOP is an acronym for a technique commonly used in DBT. It is used precisely in this sort of case when we need to pause to manage emotional responses to challenging situations without leaving the floor to our impulsivity. It's a simple (which doesn't mean easy) but effective technique. Here is how it works.

> -> Long-term strategy: Practice STOP

1. **S – Stop:** Immediately stop what you're doing, whether it's speaking, reacting, or acting impulsively. This pause gives you a moment to break the automatic response cycle. Stopping prevents you from making hasty decisions that might escalate a situation or lead to regret.
2. **T – Take a Step Back:** Mentally and physically step back from the situation. Take a deep breath, or even physically remove yourself from the environment if possible. This allows you to distance yourself from immediate emotional reactions and gain a more objective perspective.
3. **O – Observe:** Observe what's happening both internally (your emotions, thoughts, body sensations) and externally (what's going on around you). What are your feelings? What are the facts of the situation? By observing without judgment, you become more aware of the emotions driving your impulses and the broader context, allowing for a more thoughtful response.
4. **P – Proceed Mindfully**: After observing the situation, proceed with awareness and intention. What do you actually want from the situation? Choose a response that aligns with your goals and values rather than reacting

impulsively. Proceeding mindfully helps you make more thoughtful and deliberate decisions, minimizing impulsivity and working toward a solution.

Want an example? Let me tell you about Raphael. He struggled with emotional regulation during arguments with his partner, Josh. When he felt misunderstood or frustrated, his instinct was to immediately defend himself and make accusations. Josh, who tends to process emotions more slowly, was feeling overwhelmed by Raphael's intensity, leading him to withdraw from the argument. This withdrawal frustrated Raphael and led to a feedback loop. He decided to look into DBT for emotional regulation, and this is how he implemented STOP during a recent argument about forgetting to pick up a parcel:

1. **Stop**: Raphael felt his natural reaction arising when Josh pointed out he had forgotten to pick up that parcel. So he stopped talking, knowing he was going to make excuses, and it would only make things worse.
2. **Take a Step Back**: He took a deep breath and decided to sit down with a glass of cold water to ground himself.
3. **Observe**: As he slowly sipped the water, he took a moment to observe his emotions and thoughts and realized he had been super stressed at work. He also noticed that Josh was going on with cooking dinner and didn't seem angry. He wasn't trying to pick a fight.
4. **Proceed mindfully**: He calmly shared how he was feeling and what was happening at work and apologized, acknowledging Josh's disappointment in having to wait another day to get his new headphones (which were in the parcel). He invited Josh to think together about what could help him remember chores, particularly when he's stressed.

Note that STOP doesn't mean "stop and repress your emotions" or "stop and never talk about it by risk of upsetting your partner." The proceed step is just as important as stepping back, but what makes it 'mindful' is all three steps before. It might take a few goes before it starts to feel natural, but with time, like everything else, it will become second nature. If you want to practice outside of real-life situations, there is another technique worth looking at.

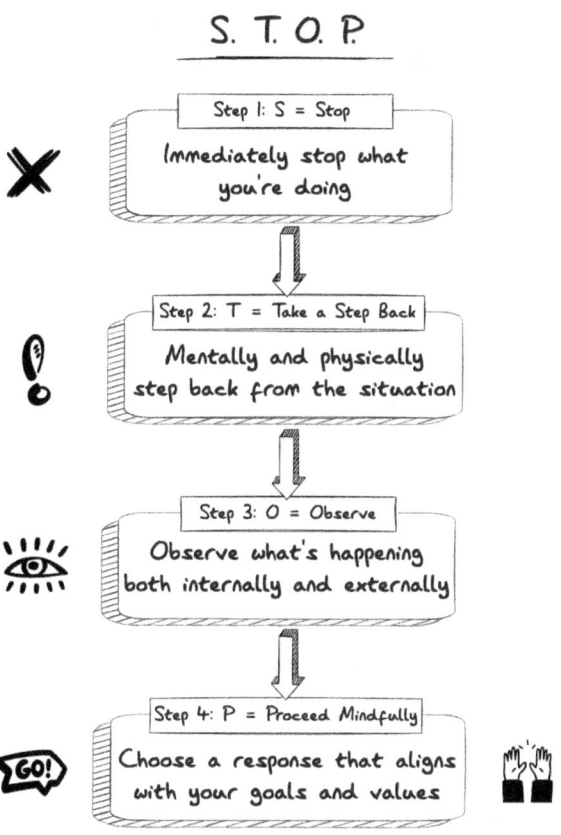

GO-NO-GO

Enter the **Go/No-Go test**—a psychological tool that helps assess and even *train* impulse control. And who doesn't like a psychological test, right? Oh, is it just me then? This one is used in research and clinical settings to measure impulse control and response inhibition, but it can also be a fantastic training tool to help us hit the brakes before our impulses take the wheel.

Here's how it works: participants are shown a series of stimuli (think letters, numbers, shapes—you know, the usual suspects). Most of the time, there's a go signal, which means you press a button as fast as possible. But every now and then, a no-go signal pops up, and the challenge is to *not* press the button. That's it—don't press the button. Just like 'stop,' it sounds simple, right? Wrong! Because there are far more go signals than no-go signals, your brain gets conditioned to react quickly, and stopping yourself becomes a lot trickier.

A 2012 Japanese study found that Go/No-Go training improves inhibitory control by enhancing activation in the right inferior frontal cortex (IFC)—a key brain region for response inhibition. So, you can actually use the Go/No-Go concept to train your brain. Apps like *Peak* and *Cognifit*, mentioned in week 2, have Go/No-Go training exercises built-in, so you can improve impulse control while playing games on your phone. Want to start training? Here is a plan.

-> Long-term strategy: Go/No-Go Training Plan

- Find an App that can measure progress and gradually increase complexity, like *CogniFit* or *Peak* mentioned.
- Train 3-5 times a week for about 15-20 minutes/day.
- Schedule when you're going to do it.
- Try pairing up with someone. It will help you stick with it. Or plan a reward for keeping at it for a month.
- Review your progress after 20 sessions (or about a month)

The real beauty of the Go/No-Go test is that it teaches your brain to pause—something that can make a massive difference in how we make everyday decisions. Whether it's stopping yourself from interrupting someone (been there), avoiding an impulsive purchase (hello, online shopping), or just pausing before reacting in a heated moment, this test helps build that STOP muscle that allows us to take a beat before acting.

3. KEEP GOING

As mentioned in the opening of this chapter, many of the techniques we've covered in previous weeks help with impulsivity and emotional regulation. So, it is time to take another look at those long-term strategies and reflect. Which ones are you already implementing? What is getting in the way? Which ones should you add?

Spoiler alert: it's not about being perfect; it's about figuring out what works for *you*.

-> Reflections: impulsivity and emotional regulation long-term strategies

Answer the questions below. They might not all be relevant, as some might refer to techniques you haven't used. Regardless, this is another opportunity for you to consider them.

Good Sleep

- *How does the quality of my sleep affect my impulsivity the next day?*

Improving my sleep habits could reduce fatigue, which often heightens impulsivity, leading to more stable and thoughtful behavior during the day.

- *What changes can I make to my sleep routine to improve sleep quality and reduce impulsive behaviors?*

If I focus on better sleep hygiene, I could experience greater mental clarity and emotional regulation, both of which are key to controlling impulsivity.

- *Am I consistently implementing good sleep hygiene practices, and what barriers prevent me from doing so?*

Getting better sleep could significantly enhance my ability to manage my impulses, as rest improves overall brain function and self-control.

Good Food

- *Have I noticed any correlation between my diet and my level of impulsivity?*

Starting to eat healthier could stabilize my mood and energy levels, reducing the likelihood of impulsive reactions due to hunger, sugar spikes, or nutrient deficiencies.

- *What foods or eating patterns seem to increase or decrease my impulsiveness?*

By paying attention to my diet, I could reduce irritability and impulsivity through balanced nutrition, and fuel my brain to make better decisions.

- *How can I adjust my diet to better support my neurological needs and reduce impulsivity?*

Adopting healthier eating habits could help regulate my brain chemistry, improving my ability to think clearly and avoid impulsive decisions.

Routines

- *Do established routines help me manage impulsivity, and how?*

Creating consistent routines could give me structure and reduce opportunities for impulsive decisions, as I would have a clear path to follow throughout the day.

- *Which parts of my daily or weekly routine are most effective in providing structure and reducing impulsive decisions?*

If I start building routines, they could serve as anchors to help me stay focused and grounded, making impulsive behavior less likely.

- *What challenges do I face in maintaining routines, and how can I address them?*

Establishing predictable routines, like Focus Zones, could help limit distractions and create a sense of stability, which may decrease impulsive tendencies.

Mindfulness

- *How has practicing mindfulness affected my awareness of impulsive thoughts or actions?*

If I haven't started yet, mindfulness could help me become more aware of my impulses before they lead to actions, giving me space to make more thoughtful decisions.

- Am I able to catch myself before acting impulsively more often since practicing mindfulness?

Mindfulness can teach me to pause and observe my thoughts without judgment, making it easier to recognize and prevent impulsive actions.

- What specific mindfulness exercises help me calm down or pause when I feel impulsive?

Starting a regular mindfulness practice could equip me with quick techniques to ground myself in the moment and reduce impulsivity.

Cognitive Behavioral Therapy (CBT)

- Have the cognitive strategies from CBT helped me in recognizing and managing impulsive behaviors?

CBT can provide me with mental tools to identify thought patterns that lead to impulsive behaviors and offer alternative ways to respond.

- What CBT techniques can I use when I notice the urge to act impulsively?

If I haven't tried CBT yet, it could help me develop strategies to pause, reflect, and redirect impulsive actions before they become problematic.

- How do I apply CBT methods in day-to-day situations that trigger impulsivity?

By starting CBT, I could learn to challenge impulsive thoughts and practice responding with more deliberate, measured actions in my daily life.

Dialectical Behavior Therapy (DBT)

- Which aspects of DBT (e.g., distress tolerance, emotional regulation) have helped me manage impulsivity?

DBT could teach me coping skills for managing intense emotions and stress, which often trigger impulsive reactions.

- *How effective have the DBT skills been in helping me think through the consequences before acting?*

If I start using DBT techniques, I could develop the ability to pause and consider the consequences of my actions, leading to better decision-making.

- *Can I identify any changes in my relationships or decision-making process due to applying DBT principles?*

Using DBT could help me improve my relationships by managing emotional impulses and communicating more effectively.

Neurofeedback

- *Have I noticed improvements in controlling impulsive behaviors since starting neurofeedback therapy?*

Trying neurofeedback could help me train my brain to self-regulate better, potentially decreasing impulsive actions by improving focus and emotional control.

- *What specific changes in my thought patterns or emotional responses can I attribute to neurofeedback sessions?*

Neurofeedback could offer me a non-invasive method to improve impulse control by strengthening brainwave patterns associated with attention and decision-making.

- *How committed am I to continuing neurofeedback, and what are my long-term goals with this therapy?*

Starting neurofeedback could help me gain a greater awareness of how my brain functions, leading to long-term improvements in managing impulsivity.

Take a moment to assess where you are and what's getting in the way because these strategies lay the foundation for emotional balance. But life doesn't always go according to plan, right? That's where the next section comes in—because sometimes, we need quick, on-the-spot techniques to regulate our emotions and impulses when things start to spiral. Plus, there are more tools you can put under your belt.

4. EMOTIONAL REGULATION TECHNIQUES

While a full course in CBT or DBT (Dialectical Behavioral Therapy) might be a great investment into your well-being, you can start small—right here, right now—with a little emotional awareness.

Thoughts Distortion

One of the things that CBT loves to target is something called cognitive distortions. These are the sneaky little tricks your brain plays on you, often blowing things out of proportion or taking you down a rabbit hole of negative thinking. You know what I'm talking about—remember that friend who canceled your plans because her pet gerbil was under the weather? Well, most likely, your brain is telling you that she's a terrible friend, and actually, now that you think of it, maybe you don't have *any* friends, and nobody has *ever* really liked you. Sound familiar? Yeah, that's classic black-and-white thinking, one of those cognitive distortions. Here are some others:

- **Overgeneralization**: Something went wrong once? Well, clearly, everything's doomed from now on.
- **Mental Filtering**: Ever focus so hard on the one negative thing that you can't even see the good stuff? That's mental filtering—where the positive gets totally drowned out by the negative.
- **Disqualifying the Positive**: Even when good things happen, you find a way to shrug them off, like "Yeah, but that doesn't count."
- **Mind Reading**: Ah, the classic "I know exactly what you're thinking, and it's definitely something bad about me."
- **Fortune Telling**: You just know things are going to go south, even though you can't see the future. It's like having a crystal ball that only predicts doom (which, for the record, is rarely accurate).

- **Catastrophizing**: Spilled coffee on your shirt? Your day is ruined, your life is over, and the world is ending!
- **Minimization**: The opposite of catastrophizing—this is when you downplay something important. That big win at work? Meh, it's no big deal.

Long-term strategy -> Emotions Tracking

The good news is that just by becoming aware of these thought patterns, we can start to loosen their grip.

1. **Write it down**: Jot down when these thoughts pop up, and reflect on them later. The simple act of writing them down can help you step back and recognize that maybe, just maybe, your brain is overreacting.
2. **Name the Trigger**: Let's layer on a bit of DBT magic. After an emotional outburst or when you catch yourself in the aftermath of one, take a moment to reflect on what just happened. This isn't about beating yourself up—it's about understanding what triggered the situation in the first place. Whatever it is, naming the trigger helps you see the situation more clearly.
3. **Name and Rate the Emotion**: Once you've figured out what triggered the outburst, the next step is to name the emotion you're feeling and rate the intensity of the emotion. Was it a simmering irritation or a full-blown volcanic eruption? By giving it a number or a level, you can start to notice patterns over time.

And those patterns? That's where the growth happens. When we become more aware of our emotional patterns, we can start to change how we respond in the future. And no, the regulation won't happen overnight. Still, we can build our emotional awareness muscle. Like any muscle, the more we exercise it, the stronger it gets.

Okay, let's be real. Even with all those tools under our belt, it can take a bit of practice, and there will still be times when emotions spiral out of control. So, how can you bring yourself down when your emotions are skyrocketing and you feel like you're on the verge of exploding, shutting down, or completely losing control? In those moments, it can be really hard to just "calm down" (as if telling ourselves that ever works, right?). What we need is something a little more tangible, something that helps us physically shift our focus away from the storm in our minds. Enter grounding techniques—simple, effective ways to bring yourself back to the present moment. Here are some of my go-to grounding techniques that work wonders when emotions are running wild.

Quick Win -> Grounding Techniques

1. **The 5-4-3-2-1 Technique**

This is probably the most popular grounding technique out there, and for good reason—it works! It's all about reconnecting with your environment through your senses. You need to find:

- **Five things you can see** - Look around and name five things you can visually spot, whether it's a plant, a pen, or a picture on the wall.
- **Four things you can touch** - Feel the texture of your clothing, a surface nearby, or even the ground beneath your feet.
- **Three things you can hear** - Listen for background sounds —the hum of a fan, distant chatter, or even birds outside.
- **Two things you can smell** - Maybe it's your cup of coffee, or you could carry a scented balm or essential oil for this purpose.
- **One thing you can taste** - If you have a drink or a mint handy, now's the time. If not, just notice the taste in your mouth.

By focusing on these physical sensations, you shift your attention away from the mental chaos and bring yourself back into the present moment—where your feet are firmly planted on the ground.

2. The Physiological Sigh

Our body does this naturally when we're stressed, but you can trigger it to help calm yourself down. Here's how it works:

- Take a deep breath in through your nose.
- Take a second, smaller inhale immediately after the first (without exhaling) to fill the lungs even more fully.
- Then, breathe out slowly and completely through your mouth, allowing your body to relax and release tension.
- Repeat as needed, typically 1-3 times, to feel calmer and more grounded.

It's a simple way to help calm your nervous system and bring yourself back to a more relaxed, focused state—especially when everything feels like it's getting a bit too much.

3. Cold Therapy

This one is even more simple but powerful. You know that feeling when something really cold or scorching hits your skin, and it's like a jolt to your system? That's what makes this technique effective. You can splash cold water on your face, grab something frozen, or even run your hands under cold water. The sensation shocks your body just enough to pull your attention away from spiraling emotions and bring you back to the present.

4. Anchoring Touch

Okay, I love this one. It's discreet and can be done anywhere, even in a meeting or with people around. This technique allows you to choose a specific physical action to "anchor" yourself in the present moment. Here are two that work for me:

- **Hand on Heart**: Simply place your hand on your heart. It's comforting, it's grounding, and it's a subtle reminder that you're here, you're present, and you're okay.
- **Hand on Skull**: Another one I love is placing my hand gently on the top of my head. It brings me right back into my body and gives me a sense of stability when my mind feels like it's running away with me.

These touches are small, but they're powerful reminders that you're still in control, even when your emotions feel like they're taking over.

5. Mental Grounding

Now, if physical techniques aren't your thing, you can also try mental grounding techniques. These involve using your mind to shift focus and calm yourself down:

- **Listing**: Try listing categories—like fruits, animals, or your favorite things. I prefer listing my favorite things because it has the added bonus of putting me in a more positive mindset.
- **Counting**: Simple but effective—counting backward from 100, for example, helps shift your focus away from racing thoughts.
- **Reciting a Poem or Singing**: If you have a favorite poem or song, repeating it (out loud or in your head) can be grounding, too. Sometimes, I'll even pair it with the hand-on-heart technique for an extra layer of calm.
- **Repeating a mantra or affirmation**: Similar to a song or a poem but with the added benefit of delivering a message. "Let Go," "I am enough" or "I have all the skills I need to deal with this" are some of the most popular ones in anxiety and highly emotional situations.

6. Mix and Match

The best part about grounding techniques? You can mix and match. Put your hand on your heart while counting backward. Or list your favorite things while you do the physiological sigh. The goal here is to find what works best for *you* and keep it in your back pocket for those moments when your emotions are way too high and you just need to come back down to earth.

Now that you've grounded yourself and brought things down a notch, it's time to take it a step further with some self-soothing strategies. This is where we learn how to comfort ourselves—without relying on someone else to calm us down or waiting for the situation to magically improve. Self-soothing is powerful as it puts control in our hands. It's all about creating a sense of peace and comfort for yourself by engaging your senses. Think about what feels good for *you*. There's no "right" way to do this—it's whatever brings you comfort. Let's break it down by senses.

Quick Win -> Self-soothing strategies

1. Touch

Maybe it's sinking into a warm bath, curling up under your duvet, or wrapping yourself in a weighted blanket. If you've got a pet, snuggling up with them can be the perfect way to relax and release oxytocin, a neurotransmitter that can regulate our emotions. You can also give yourself a little self-massage—feet, hands, shoulders, wherever you need it. Or simply change into your most comfortable clothes that make you feel like a cozy cocoon. I famously invested in a onesie last winter and haven't looked back.

2. Taste

Okay, when we're stressed, it's easy to reach for something sugary or indulgent. But let's aim for something soothing that won't make us crash later. Try sipping a warm drink like herbal tea or a cold, refreshing glass of water. The idea is to give your taste buds something gentle and satisfying without relying on that giant tub of ice cream (tempting as it may be!).

3. Sight

Surround yourself with things that make you feel good. You could look at pictures of happy memories—whether it's from a holiday, time with friends, or even a favorite place. If you're into something more meditative, stare at a flickering candle, a lava lamp, or a fireplace. Watching those simple, soothing movements can be mesmerizing in the best way possible.

4. Smell

Smell is an incredibly powerful sense when it comes to self-soothing. Speaking of flickering lights, if you've got a scented candle you love, light it up! You can also use scented lotions, essential oils, or even just your favorite soap. Inhale deeply, and let the smell wash over you.

5. Sound

Music is probably one of the most universally comforting things out there. Whether it's soft, slow tunes or something more upbeat, pick music that calms you down. Nature sounds are also a great option—think of the sound of running water, rain, or birds chirping. If listening live is not an option, you can even listen to them as white noise. If you're into ASMR (that soothing, tingly audio experience), go for that, or maybe you prefer total silence, in which case you could invest in noise-canceling headphones or earplugs.

6. Mix and Match Your Senses

Just like grounding techniques, you don't have to pick just one sense. Combine them! Play your favorite music while you give yourself a foot massage with a beautifully scented lotion. Or wrap up in a cozy blanket while sipping on a warm tea and watching the flicker of a candle. It's all about finding what works best for you and creating a soothing environment that helps you reset and recharge. The key is to find what makes *you* feel calm and centered.

These techniques can bring quick relief, but they're also building blocks for long-term emotional resilience. You can use self-soothing strategies and grounding techniques as comfort after any emotional moment but also make them part of your everyday life as a preventative strategy. With practice, you'll find that small shifts in awareness and action can make a big difference in how you respond to emotional triggers.

FINAL THOUGHTS

We've all been there—where one small trigger suddenly feels like a tidal wave of emotion, and impulsivity takes the wheel before rationale even has a chance to chime in. Living with ADHD means we experience emotions at full volume and impulsivity. That's the reckless driver tutting the horn loudly, pushing us to react *now* before we've even had time to think.

But here's the thing: we don't have to be at the mercy of these knee-jerk reactions. As we've explored throughout this chapter, emotional regulation and impulsivity are deeply intertwined with our executive function, and thankfully, these can be worked on.

From long-term strategies like CBT, DBT, and mindfulness to quick emergency techniques like grounding exercises and self-soothing, we now have tools to help us create space between stimulus and response.

We now know that while impulsivity might never entirely disappear, we can manage it, understand its triggers, and build healthier habits to respond in ways that align more with who we want to be. So, as you wrap up Week 7, take a moment to reflect on the strategies that are already working for you and the areas where you can still improve. It is *your* toolkit, and you'll continue to refine and expand it over time.

KEY TAKEAWAYS

- **Impulsivity and emotional dysregulation are deeply connected to our executive functioning.** With our working memory failing to remind us of past experiences and a lack of cognitive flexibility locking us into one emotional lens, we often react more intensely than the situation calls for. It's not just those emotional roller coasters out of nowhere—impulsivity sneaks into decision-making, reactions, and even the small stuff in everyday life.
- **Impulsivity isn't always obvious.** It's not just interrupting conversations or blurting things out; it can be those subtle moments when you say "yes" to something without thinking it through or make a decision on the fly that you regret later. It's the impulse buys, the spontaneous emotional reactions, or all the things that stack up and leave us wondering, "Why did I do that?"
- **Understanding why you want to manage your impulsivity is the real motivator.** This isn't about being 'polite' or doing things just to fit in. It's about feeling better afterward, avoiding regret, and aligning your reactions with who you actually want to be.
- **The journey so far has armed you with tools you can already use.** Remember the strategies from previous weeks, from good sleep to mindfulness? They are all stepping stones that strengthen your ability to pause, reflect, and act

with intention when emotions and impulsivity threaten to take over.
- **STOP**: This simple DBT technique—Stop, Take a Step Back, Observe, and Proceed Mindfully—can stop those knee-jerk reactions in their tracks and give you space to react with intention. Go/No-Go is like a mini workout for your brain to help you hit pause before impulsivity takes over.
- **CBT and DBT are long-term strategies**: CBT helps you call out those sneaky cognitive distortions, while DBT gives you the tools to ride out those intense emotions and handle them without jumping straight into action.
- **Grounding techniques and self-soothing are lifesavers when emotions start to spiral.** Whether it's the classic 5-4-3-2-1 trick or something as simple as a cold splash of water, grounding brings you back into the present and helps you regain control in the heat of the moment. Self-soothing gives you the power to create comfort through touch, taste, sound, and more. These tools can provide in-the-moment relief while building long-term emotional resilience.

in conclusion

Well, here we are, at the end of the book—or should I say, at the beginning of your next chapter? If you've made it this far (and stayed with me through all the metaphors, references, and the occasional corny joke), congratulations! You've done more than just read a book; you've dug deep into understanding how your brain works, how ADHD and executive function impact your daily life, and, more importantly, you've begun to assemble a toolkit that will help you thrive in ways that make sense for you.

You've got a variety of tools at your disposal now—some shiny and new, others a bit more familiar. But the important thing is, you have options, as there's no one-size-fits-all solution when it comes to managing ADHD and strengthening executive function.

Remember how we started our journey together? In the first week, we laid the groundwork by understanding the connection between ADHD and executive function. You discovered how working memory, cognitive flexibility, and inhibitory control form the pillars of executive function and why ADHD loves to throw a wrench into its smooth operation and meddle with time, focus, organization, and impulse control. You also started to identify what can help and what can make it worse (yes, I'm looking at you, stress).

With that insight, you took that all-important audit of your needs. You identified where ADHD hits you hardest—mapping the journey ahead and embracing the idea that your brain simply works differently. That's not a flaw—it's just a fact. With that, you opened the door to change, armed with the hope of neuroplasticity and a growth mindset.

From there, you stepped into the brain gym and started to exercise those cognitive skills with apps and exercises. You learned that sleep is a game changer, that good nutrition fuels your focus, and that exercise isn't just for your body—it boosts your brain, too. In short, taking care of your body isn't just "self-care fluff" but integral to managing ADHD. And yes, you've got the breathing exercises and mindfulness practices to back it up. They're not just tools for reducing stress (though that's a huge benefit)—they help you tap into clarity.

Then, we got into the heart of cognitive flexibility. This wasn't just about shifting gears between tasks but about handling life's inevitable changes and frustrations without spiraling. You've learned how to practice flexibility and incorporate mindfulness in everyday life. We also looked at other long-term strategies like reframing your thoughts with CBT or building emotional resilience with DBT. These tools have empowered you to bend without breaking when things don't go to plan—and they will, because life and ADHD are both unpredictable like that.

By the time we hit week four, we moved from internal to external spaces. We tackled the messiness that can feel overwhelming for us folks with ADHD. But this wasn't about striving for a Pinterest-perfect life. Nope. This was about finding systems that work for *you*—where functionality takes the lead and aesthetics play a distant second. From decluttering and creating zones to reducing decision fatigue with minimalism, you began to see how small changes in your space could lead to big improvements in how you feel. And when we talked about losing things? You realized that chaos doesn't have to be your norm. Simple routines and mindful transitions can reduce the number of "Where did I put that?" moments.

As we hit the slippery slope of time management, we saw that Time Blindness is real and makes time either drag on forever or disappear when we hyperfocus. But with tools like timers, external reminders, and flexible routines that fit your energy levels, you're not just managing time—you're mastering your relationship with it. Through the spoon theory, you've learned to pace yourself with energy in mind, avoiding the dangers of hyperfocus burnout and recognizing that it's not just about the hours in a day but how much mental and emotional energy you can give to each task.

As a newly proclaimed master of space and time, you were ready to tackle productivity. You discovered that healthy productivity for ADHD brains is not about grinding harder; it's about working smarter. We flipped the script on traditional productivity hacks that can often backfire, leaving you more burned out than accomplished. Instead, you've picked up strategies that honor your unique energy levels, like creating focus zones to eliminate distractions and make the most of your productive moments. Of course, we looked at prioritization techniques, but most importantly, you've come to see productivity as a balance of focus, energy management, and mindful rest. Hyperfocus, daydreaming, and even the art of saying "no" became tools for success, not stumbling blocks.

And finally, with all these new tools in the background, we were ready to look at emotional dysregulation and impulsivity straight in the eyes and identify their deep tie to executive function. Let's be honest, emotions can run wild when ADHD is involved. Whether it's snapping at someone in a meeting or making impulsive decisions that leave you feeling embarrassed, you've now learned how to create space between stimulus and response. Tools like the STOP technique, grounding exercises, and mindfulness gave you the ability to hit pause, reflect, and choose how to respond rather than reacting on autopilot. Emotional regulation is no longer just a concept—it's something you can actively work on with tools that allow you to ride those emotional waves instead of being swept away by them.

So, what's next? Well, the truth is, this journey doesn't have a clear endpoint. Life and ADHD aren't static—they're constantly shifting, but you've gathered an arsenal of tools and strategies, and you're ready to continue the work. You'll have good days, bad days, and everything in between. The beauty of everything you've learned here is that it's adaptable. You can pick up new tools, toss the old ones that no longer serve you, and keep evolving as your preferences and life circumstances change. And if you need help implementing them and figuring out which ones work best for you, get in touch, and let's chat about my mentoring program.

The most important takeaway? You've done the work to understand yourself better, and that self-awareness is the most powerful tool in your kit. The strategies you've learned will help you live with more intention, more clarity, and more compassion for yourself. So, as you move forward, remember to be kind to yourself. There will be days when everything clicks, and then there will be days when it feels like you're right back at square one. But here's the truth: you're not. Every bit of self-awareness you've gained, every tool you've practiced, builds on itself. Progress with ADHD isn't linear, but it is real.

As we part ways (at least for now), know this: you're not alone. You've done incredible work to get here, and the journey doesn't stop now. Life with ADHD is a process, not a destination. Keep going. Keep evolving. Keep showing up for yourself.

So, what's next? Well, that's entirely up to you.

resources

Apps

Yoga Nidra: *InsightTimer*
Hydration: *My Hydration, Drink Water*
Interactive Exercise: *Zombie, Run!*
Brain Training: *N-Back, Elevate, BrainHQ, CogniFit, Mind Games, Luminosity, Peak*
Meditation & Mindfulness: *Balance, Headspace, InsightTimer*
Time management: *TickTick, Motion, Toggl Track*

Websites

Alcohol Use Disorders Identification Test (AUDIT): auditscreen.org
Brain Workshop: brainworkshop.sourceforge.net
The Biofeedback Certification International Alliance (BCIA): bcia.org
The International Society for Neurofeedback & Research (ISNR): isnr.org
Myndlift: myndlift.com
Neuroptimal: neuroptimal.com
DBT-Linehan Board of Certification: dbt-lbc.org

Estelle Rose: estelle-rose.com

Books

Bailey, C. (2018). *Hyperfocus: How to Be More Productive in a World of Distraction.* Random House Canada.

Rose, E. (2023). *Brain Boosting Food for Women with ADHD: Improve Concentration, Motivation, Mood and Memory.* Rosali Publishing.

Rose, E. (2024). *Empowering Books for Women with ADHD. 2 in 1: Guide and Workbook. The complete toolkit to improve executive function, self-regulation, and self-acceptance.* Rosali Publishing.

Zylowska, L., & Siegel, D. J., MD. (2012). *The Mindfulness Prescription for Adult ADHD: An Eight-step Program for Strengthening Attention, Managing Emotions, and Achieving Your Goals.* Shambhala Publications.

IT'S NOT TOO LATE

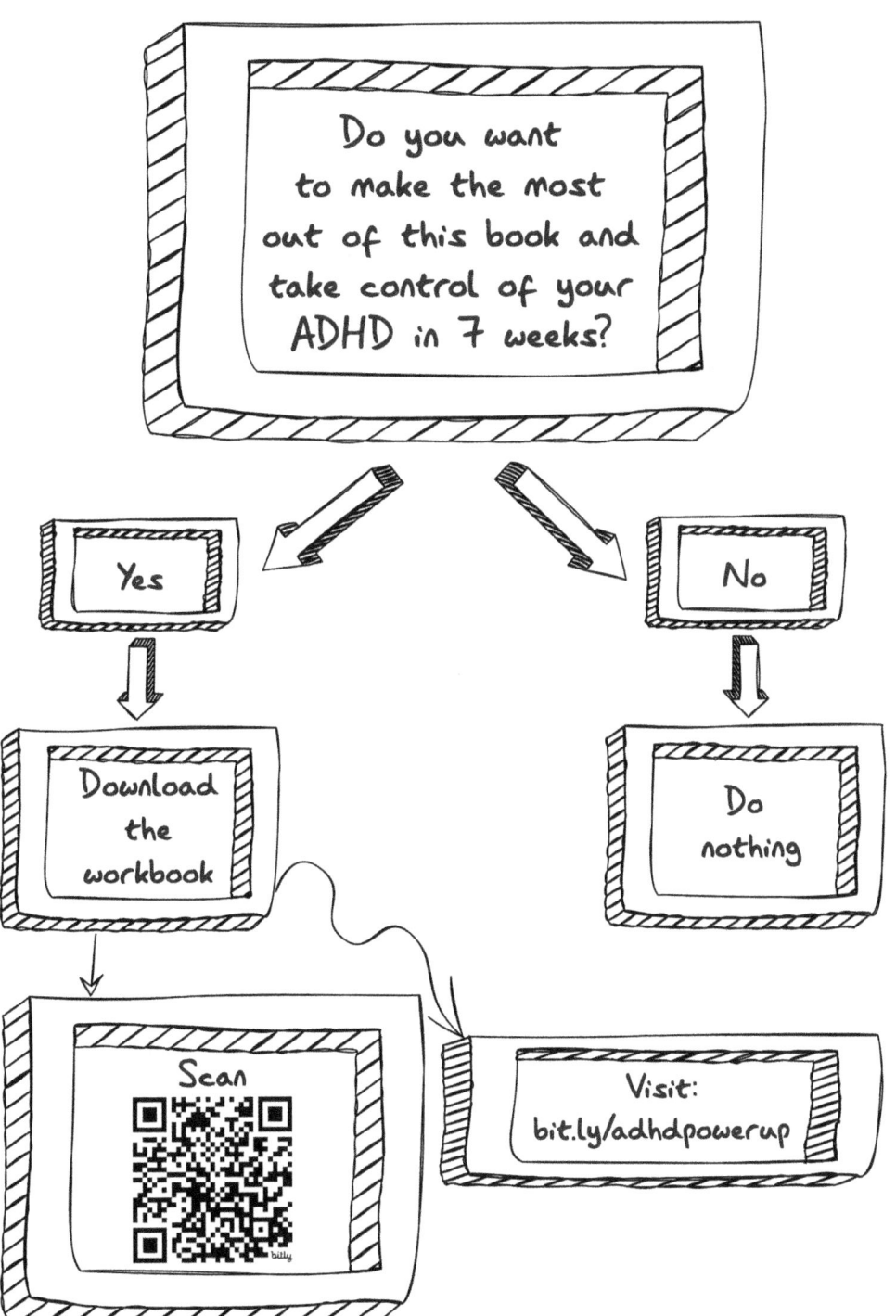

about the author

Estelle Rose is the author of *The Empowering ADHD Workbook for Women*, *Empowered Women with ADHD*, and *Brain-Boosting Food for Women with ADHD*.

With an infectious passion for helping women thrive, Estelle's mission is simple yet profound: to empower women with ADHD to better understand themselves, embrace their strengths, and lead fulfilling lives.

Diagnosed later in life, Estelle brings a personal and empathetic perspective to her work. Her own journey of navigating ADHD led her to delve deeply into fields like psychology, neuroscience, behavioral therapy, nutrition, and mindfulness practices. Along the way, she became a certified coach, DBT and EFT practitioner.

With a compassionate tone and practical strategies, her writing feels like a conversation with a trusted friend, offering readers tools to manage their symptoms, embrace their unique potential, and live with confidence.

If you're looking for more personalized support, Estelle also offers workshops and one-on-one mentoring tailored to meet your needs. Whether you're just beginning your ADHD journey or looking for fresh ways to thrive, Estelle is here to guide and inspire you.

Whether through her books, workshops, coaching or mentoring, Estelle is always happy to connect with fellow ADHDers to explore how she can work with you to create positive, lasting changes in your life.

You can connect on www.estelle-rose.com

also by estelle rose

Hey there! If Adult ADHD Executive Function 7-Week Power-Up gave you a spark of hope and momentum, I've got more where that came from. Let me introduce you to a few of my other books—think of them as the squad that's got your back, ready to help you tackle life with ADHD in the most practical, empowering, and sometimes laugh-out-loud way.

The Empowering ADHD Workbook for Women: Embrace Your Brilliance Without the Burnout

This one's a game-changer if you're ready to dig deep and tackle the stuff that really holds us back—think self-esteem, confidence, and those never-ending racing thoughts. It's packed with hands-on tools, downloadable trackers, and beautifully illustrated pages designed for our neurospicy brains (same illustrator as Empowered Women With ADHD—more on that in a sec). Plus, we're talking career and finance advice, emotional regulation, and clutter-busting tips you can actually stick to. If the current book is about getting your executive functions humming, this one's about reconnecting with you—your confidence, your calm, and your power.

EMPOWERED WOMEN WITH ADHD: UNLOCK YOUR FULL POTENTIAL WITH PROVEN TOOLS AND STRATEGIES

This one's like your candid, no-judgment BFF who gets what it's like to live on the ADHD rollercoaster. We're slowing down the racing thoughts, setting boundaries (without the guilt), and creating space to thrive at work and in relationships. The illustrations are back, too—just as fun and supportive as before. Whether you're feeling stuck in hyperfocus or overwhelmed by hyper-fatigue, this book will meet you where you are and help you make ADHD work for you instead of against you.

BRAIN-BOOSTING FOODS FOR WOMEN WITH ADHD: NOURISH YOUR FOCUS, MOOD, AND ENERGY

Let's talk about food (and yes, snacks). If brain fog and low energy are slowing you down, this book has your back with a nutrition-focused guide to ADHD-friendly eating. You'll find affordable, accessible ingredients, quick recipes (we're talking under 15 minutes), and week-by-week meal plans that make eating for focus and clarity a breeze. Say goodbye to that "traffic jam" feeling in your brain and hello to more energy, better mood, and recipes you'll actually want to make.

I wrote these books because I've been in the trenches, too—trying to juggle all the things while feeling like I'm constantly losing my grip. If you're ready for practical tools, a little bit of laughter, and a whole lot of *you've got this* energy, these books are here to help.

Let's keep this momentum going—your brilliance is just getting started.

bibliography

Abdulghani, A., Poghosyan, M., Mehren, A., Philipsen, A., & Anderzhanova, E. (2023). Neuroplasticity to autophagy cross-talk in a therapeutic effect of physical exercises and irisin in ADHD. *Frontiers in Molecular Neuroscience*, 15. https://doi.org/10.3389/fnmol.2022.997054.

Angelou, Maya, *The Art of Fiction No. 119* (2021) *The Paris Review*. https://www.theparisreview.org/interviews/2279/the-art-of-fiction-no-119-maya-angelou?src=longreads

Barra, S., Grub, A., Roesler, M., Retz-Junginger, P., Philipp, F., & Retz, W. (2021). The role of stress coping strategies for life impairments in ADHD. *Journal of Neural Transmission* (Vienna, Austria: 1996), 128(7), 981–992. https://doi.org/10.1007/s00702-021-02311-5

Burnette, J., Babij, A., Oddo, L., & Knouse, L. (2020). Self-Regulation Mindsets: Relationship to Coping, Executive Functioning, and ADHD. *Journal of Social and Clinical Psychology*, 39, 101-116. https://doi.org/10.1521/jscp.2020.39.02.101.

Combs, M., Canu, W., Broman-Fulks, J., Rocheleau, C., & Nieman, D. (2015). Perceived Stress and ADHD Symptoms in Adults. *Journal of Attention Disorders*, 19, 425 - 434. https://doi.org/10.1177/1087054712459558.

Covey, S. R. (2004). *The 7 Habits of Highly Effective People: Powerful Lessons in Personal Change*. Simon and Schuster.

Dai, C., Zhang, Y., Cai, X., Peng, Z., Zhang, L., Shao, Y., & Wang, C. (2020). Effects of Sleep Deprivation on Working Memory: Change in Functional Connectivity Between the Dorsal Attention, Default Mode, and Fronto-Parietal Networks. *Frontiers in Human Neuroscience*, 14. https://doi.org/10.3389/fnhum.2020.00360.

Deepeshwar, S., & Budhi, R. (2022). Slow yoga breathing improves mental load in working memory performance and cardiac activity among yoga practitioners. *Frontiers in Psychology*, 13. https://doi.org/10.3389/fpsyg.2022.968858.

Dotare, M., Bader, M., Mesrobian, S., Asai, Y., Villa, A., & Lintas, A. (2020). Attention Networks in ADHD Adults after Working Memory Training with a Dual n-Back Task. *Brain Sciences*, 10. https://doi.org/10.3390/brainsci10100715.

Hirose, S., Chikazoe, J., Watanabe, T., Jimura, K., Kunimatsu, A., Abe, O., Ohtomo, K., Miyashita, Y., & Konishi, S. (2012). Efficiency of Go/No-Go Task Performance Implemented in the Left Hemisphere. *The Journal of Neuroscience*, 32, 9059 - 9065. https://doi.org/10.1523/JNEUROSCI.0540-12.2012.

Holtmann, M., Sonuga-Barke, E., Cortese, S., & Brandeis, D. (2014). Neurofeedback for ADHD: a review of current evidence. *Child and adolescent psychiatric clinics of North America*, 23 4, 789-806. https://doi.org/10.1016/j.chc.2014.05.006.

Fargason, R., Fobian, A., Hablitz, L., Paul, J., White, B., Cropsey, K., & Gamble, K. (2017). Correcting delayed circadian phase with bright light therapy predicts improvement in ADHD symptoms: A pilot study.. *Journal of psychiatric research*, 91, 105-110. https://doi.org/10.1016/j.jpsychires.2017.03.004.

Kooij, J., Bijlenga, D., Brown, G., Someren, E., , N., Streiner, D., & , M. (2014). High Prevalence of Self-Reported Photophobia in Adult ADHD. *Frontiers in Neurology*, 5. https://doi.org/10.3389/fneur.2014.00256.

Mehren, A., Özyurt, J., Lam, A., Brandes, M., Müller, H., Thiel, C., & Philipsen, A.

(2019). Acute Effects of Aerobic Exercise on Executive Function and Attention in Adult Patients With ADHD. *Frontiers in Psychiatry*, 10. https://doi.org/10.3389/fpsyt.2019.00132.

Mitchell, J. C., Zylowska, L., & Kollins, S. H. (2015). *Mindfulness Meditation Training for Attention-Deficit/Hyperactivity Disorder in Adulthood: Current Empirical Support, Treatment Overview, and Future Directions*. Cognitive and Behavioral Practice, 22(2), 172–191. https://doi.org/10.1016/j.cbpra.2014.10.002

Morgensterns, E., Alfredsson, J., Hirvikoski, T., & Hirvikoski, T. (2016). Structured skills training for adults with ADHD in an outpatient psychiatric context: an open feasibility trial. *ADHD Attention Deficit and Hyperactivity Disorders*, 8, 101-111. https://doi.org/10.1007/s12402-015-0182-1.

Ptáček, R., Weissenberger, S., Braaten, E., Klicperová-Baker, M., Goetz, M., Raboch, J., Vňuková, M., & Stefano, G. (2019). Clinical Implications of the Perception of Time in Attention Deficit Hyperactivity Disorder (ADHD): A Review. *Medical Science Monitor: International Medical Journal of Experimental and Clinical Research*, 25, 3918 - 3924. https://doi.org/10.12659/MSM.914225.

Poissant, H., Moreno, A., Potvin, S., & Mendrek, A. (2020). A Meta-analysis of Mindfulness-Based Interventions in Adults with Attention-Deficit Hyperactivity Disorder: Impact on ADHD Symptoms, Depression, and Executive Functioning. *Mindfulness*, 11, 2669 - 2681. https://doi.org/10.1007/s12671-020-01458-8.

Raz, S., & Leykin, D. (2015). Psychological and cortisol reactivity to experimentally induced stress in adults with ADHD. *Psychoneuroendocrinology*, 60, 7-17. https://doi.org/10.1016/j.psyneuen.2015.05.008.

Salavert, J., Ramos-Quiroga, J., Moreno-Alcázar, A., Caseras, X., Palomar, G., Raduà, J., Bosch, R., Salvador, R., McKenna, P., Casas, M., & Pomarol-Clotet, E. (2018). Functional Imaging Changes in the Medial Prefrontal Cortex in Adult ADHD. *Journal of Attention Disorders*, 22, 679 - 693. https://doi.org/10.1177/1087054715611492.

Schönenberg, M., Wiedemann, E., Schneidt, A., Scheeff, J., Logemann, A., Keune, P. M., & Hautzinger, M. (2017). Neurofeedback, sham neurofeedback, and cognitive-behavioural group therapy in adults with attention-deficit hyperactivity disorder: a triple-blind, randomised, controlled trial. *The Lancet. Psychiatry*, 4(9), 673–684. https://doi.org/10.1016/S2215-0366(17)30291-2

Sumantry, D., & Stewart, K. E. (2021). *Meditation, Mindfulness, and Attention: a Meta-analysis*. Mindfulness, 12(6), 1332–1349. https://doi.org/10.1007/s12671-021-01593-w

Vela, R. (2016). *Neuroanatomical basis of emotional dysregulation in children and adults with ADHD*. European Psychiatry, 33. https://doi.org/10.1016/J.EURPSY.2016.01.1294

Wang, Y., Zuo, C., Xu, Q., Hao, L., & Zhang, Y. (2021). Attention-deficit/hyperactivity disorder is characterized by a delay in subcortical maturation. *Progress in Neuro-Psychopharmacology and Biological Psychiatry*, 104, 110044. https://doi.org/10.1016/j.pnpbp.2020.110044

Wasserstein, J., Stefanatos, G., & Solanto, M. (2023). 2 Perimenopause, Menopause and ADHD. *Journal of the International Neuropsychological Society*, 29, 881 - 881. https://doi.org/10.1017/s1355617723010846.

Watson, N., Badr, M., Belenky, G., Bliwise, D., Buxton, O., Buysse, D., Dinges, D., Gangwisch, J., Grandner, M., Kushida, C., Malhotra, R., Martin, J., Patel, S., Quan, S., Tasali, E., Twery, M., Croft, J., Maher, E., Barrett, J., Thomas, S., & Heald, J. (2015). Recommended Amount of Sleep for a Healthy Adult: A Joint Consensus

Statement of the American Academy of Sleep Medicine and Sleep Research Society.. *Journal of Clinical Sleep Medicine: JCSM : official publication of the American Academy of Sleep Medicine,* 11 6, 591-2 . https://doi.org/10.5664/jcsm.4758.

www.ingramcontent.com/pod-product-compliance
Lightning Source LLC
Chambersburg PA
CBHW071713020426
42333CB00017B/2255